MY FIRST BIBLE REFERENCE

BIBLE MINUTES FOR BOYS

200 GOTTA-KNOW PEOPLE, PLACES, IDEAS & MORE

BARBOUR **kidz**
A Division of Barbour Publishing

CONTENTS

THERE'S NO MORE IMPORTANT BOOK THAN THE BIBLE.

THIS BOOK MAKES LEARNING THE BIBLE FUN AND EASY!

. . . .

This "first Bible reference" was created especially for boys ages 6 and up. Flip through the following pages, and you'll be introduced to some of the Bible's most important names, places, and ideas.

Each of the 200 entries can be easily read and understood in 60 seconds or less. These key bits of knowledge will help you see what God's Word is all about! Plus, if you want to go further, each entry includes a "Learn More" reference that you can look up in your own Bible.

Here's what you'll find inside:

People: 50 important men and women, from Aaron through Zacharias, including—of course—Jesus, the most important Person ever.

Places: 31 key nations, cities, towns, rivers, lakes, and other spots you should know—in alphabetical order from Antioch of Syria through Tarsus.

Events: 47 history-making moments—in order from the Fall of Satan through Heaven Comes to Earth.

Ideas: 42 "theological concepts" (to use a big phrase) that God considered important enough to place in the Bible—from Baptism through Worship.

Names of God: 30 of the most interesting and important names of the Trinity—God the Father, Jesus Christ the Son, and the Holy Spirit.

You'll love the interesting facts and details from scripture, all in a colorful, take-anywhere package. (By the way, when you see a name or word printed in color, that means it has its own entry in the book—be sure to look it up!) *Bible Minutes for Boys* will fire up a lifelong love of learning God's Word!

AARON

*Aaron spoke all the words which the Lord
had spoken to Moses. Then he did all the
special works for the people to see.*
EXODUS 4:30

Aaron was the brother of **Moses** and Miriam. **God** called Aaron to be the spokesman for Moses to lead the Hebrews out of Egypt. Pharaoh did not want to let the Hebrews leave Egypt, but through God's power, Aaron stretched out his staff to bring some of the ten plagues against the land (Exodus 7:19).

Aaron and another man, Hur, helped Moses hold up his hands to bring victory during a battle in the wilderness. But Aaron did not always honor God with his actions. When Moses was on **Mount Sinai** getting the Ten Commandments from God, Aaron allowed the people to make a golden calf and worship it as a false god. God showed his **grace** to Aaron and did not punish him. Aaron repented of his **sin** and later became the first high priest of **Israel**.

LEARN MORE: Exodus 7:8–20

ABEL

*But Abel brought a gift of the first-born of
his flocks and of the fat parts. The Lord
showed favor to Abel and his gift.*
GENESIS 4:4

. . . .

Abel was the second son of **Adam** and **Eve**. He had an
older brother named **Cain**. In Genesis 4 we read that
Abel was a shepherd and Cain worked in the fields. One
day, both Abel and Cain brought offerings to the Lord.
Cain brought some fruits from the garden as an **offering**
to **God** and Abel brought the best of his flock.

Cain's offering made God angry, but God was happy
with Abel's offering.

Cain was so angry that God did not take his offering
that he acted out in anger against his brother Abel and
killed him in a field.

The book of Hebrews tells us that Abel's offering
proved his faith and his good character (Hebrews 11:4).

. . . .

LEARN MORE: Genesis 4:1–25

ABRAHAM

*Now the Lord said to Abram, "Leave your
country, your family and your father's house,
and go to the land that I will show you.*
GENESIS 12:1

You may have heard Abraham called "Father Abraham."
This nickname is because God promised Abraham that
he would be the father of a great nation, with children
and grandchildren and great-grandchildren who would
be as many as the stars in the sky or grains of sand on
the beach. This promise confused Abraham and his wife,
though, because God promised this to him when he didn't
have *any* children!

It took many years, but God did give Abraham and his
wife Sarah a son, Isaac. God would later test Abraham's
faith by asking him to sacrifice Isaac. Abraham trusted
God and showed his faith by obeying. But God's angel
did not let Abraham sacrifice Isaac and provided a ram
to be sacrificed instead.

LEARN MORE: Genesis 21:1–8

PEOPLE

ADAM

*Then the Lord God made man from the dust
of the ground. And He breathed into his nose
the breath of life. Man became a living being.*
GENESIS 2:7

Adam was the first human to be created. God had created the earth, moon, stars, sun, animals, and all living things by speaking. But on the last day of creation, God took the dust from the ground and breathed His breath into it to create a man, Adam.

God made Adam in charge of the Garden of Eden and all its animals and plants. Adam had the job of naming all of the things he saw in the garden. Can you imagine coming up with new names for animals and plants? It was a big job for just one man. God saw that Adam needed a partner and God created Eve. Together they walked with God in the Garden until they sinned by eating the fruit the serpent gave them.

LEARN MORE: Genesis 2

AMOS

These are the words of Amos, a shepherd of Tekoa, which he received in special dreams about Israel two years before the earth shook.

AMOS 1:1

. . . .

In the Bible, we see that God often calls people who seem unfit for the job of prophet, priest, king, queen, or leader. He chooses humble shepherds, men who have trouble speaking, and teen girls. Amos was one of these surprising choices. He was a shepherd and farmer who God called to be a prophet to the people of Israel.

God gave Amos dreams and visions about what Israel was doing wrong and how they would be punished. Amos wanted the people to take care of the poor and only worship the one true God instead of idols and false gods. Amos was bold in his faith.

. . . .

LEARN MORE: Book of Amos

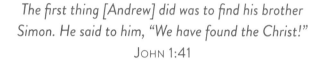

ANDREW

The first thing [Andrew] did was to find his brother
Simon. He said to him, "We have found the Christ!"
JOHN 1:41

Andrew was a follower of John the Baptist, and he believed that the Messiah had come to forgive the sins of
the people. When John the Baptist introduced Andrew
to Jesus, he immediately began to follow Him. Andrew
had faith and introduced others to Jesus. The first person
he told about Jesus was his brother, Simon Peter.

Later, Andrew told Jesus about a boy who had
brought his lunch to a place where many people had
gathered. Jesus multiplied the boy's loaves and fish to
feed the hungry crowd in a miracle that would be known
as the feeding of the five thousand.

LEARN MORE: John 6:1–11

BARNABAS

Then Barnabas took him to the missionaries.
He told them that Saul had seen the Lord on the road.
He told them also how the Lord had spoken to Saul
and how he had preached without fear in
Damascus in the name of Jesus.
ACTS 9:27

. . . .

Many people know of Paul from the Bible, but not as many know of Barnabas, the man who was a guide to Paul. In his past, Paul had killed people because they loved and followed Jesus. But Barnabas knew that Paul had changed his life and now allowed the Holy Spirit to control him.

Barnabas brought Paul along on his missionary journeys and together they told others about the Gospel of Jesus Christ. They faced many hard times together before they went their separate ways. But God used Barnabas to help train Paul. Because of Barnabas, others who had been afraid of Paul earlier now knew that he was a new person because of Jesus.

. . . .

LEARN MORE: Acts 11:19–26

BARTIMAEUS

[Bartimaeus] heard that Jesus of Nazareth was passing by. He began to speak with a loud voice, saying, "Jesus, Son of David, take pity on me!"
MARK 10:47

Bartimaeus was a blind beggar from the city of Jericho. He was sitting by the road asking for money when Jesus passed by. He had heard about Jesus' miracles and healing power. So Bartimaeus yelled out through the crowd to get Jesus' attention.

Some people standing nearby told him to stop yelling. But Bartimaeus shouted even louder so that he could be heard.

Jesus heard the blind man and called him over. When Jesus asked what he wanted, Bartimaeus said, "Lord, I want to see!" Jesus healed Bartimaeus's blindness with the words, "Go! Your faith has healed you." Bartimaeus then became a follower of Jesus.

LEARN MORE: Mark 10:46–52

BOAZ

Then Boaz said to Ruth, "Be careful to listen, my daughter. Do not go to gather grain in another field. Do not leave this one. But stay here with my women who gather grain."

RUTH 2:8

. . . .

Boaz was a rich man who owned many fields. One day, a foreign woman named **Ruth** came to work in his field to get food for herself and her mother-in-law, Naomi. Naomi and Ruth had returned to **Bethlehem**, where Naomi had grown up, after her husband and sons died. One of her sons had been married to Ruth.

Boaz allowed Ruth to work in his fields and he protected her from harm. After some time had passed, Boaz and Ruth were married and had a son. Their son, Obed, would later become the grandfather to David, who became king of Israel.

. . . .

LEARN MORE: Ruth 2

CAIN

Then the Lord said to Cain, "Where is Abel your brother?" And he said, "I do not know. Am I my brother's keeper?"
GENESIS 4:9

. . . .

Cain was the oldest son of Adam and Eve. He was the first person ever to be born on earth! But, sadly, he is also remembered as the first person who acted in violence. Cain killed his brother Abel because he was jealous of him. Abel's offering of the best animals of his flock was accepted by God. Cain's offering of fruit from his fields was not.

God punished Cain for his violence by sending him away from his family and home.

. . . .

LeARN MORe: Genesis 4:1–17

CALEB

Then Caleb told the people in front of Moses to be quiet. And he said, "Let us go up at once and take the land. For we are well able to take it in battle."
NUMBERS 13:30

God promised **Moses** and the Israelites that they would enter the Promised Land of **Canaan.** So Moses sent spies into the land to watch the people who already lived in the land. Twelve spies went into the land. Ten of them returned saying that the enemy was too tough for them to defeat. Only Caleb and **Joshua** believed that God was bigger than the armies there. They had **faith** that since God promised the land to them, He would keep His promise.

Because the Israelites didn't believe God, He punished them by making them wander in the desert for forty more years. At the end of that time, Joshua and Caleb were the only original Israelites allowed to enter the Promised Land.

LEARN MORE: Deuteronomy 1:19–40

DANIEL

So the king had Daniel brought in and thrown into the place where lions were kept. The king said to Daniel, "May your God, Whom you are faithful to serve, save you."
DANIEL 6:16

When Daniel was young, he was taken away by the Babylonian king, Nebuchadnezzar. Daniel and his friends, Shadrach, Meshach, and Abednego, chose to not eat the king's fancy food or drink his wine. They asked to eat vegetables and drink water instead. Before long, they were healthier and stronger than the other boys in the palace. This pleased King Nebuchadnezzar.

Daniel continued to show his faith through the years. Some evil men in the new king's court told the king to make a law saying nobody could worship God or pray to Him. But Daniel kept praying to God, even when it was against the law. He was punished by being thrown into a den of lions. Because of his faith and God's protection, Daniel was not harmed. This miracle caused King Darius to worship God and declare His power in front of the nation.

LEARN MORE: Daniel 6:28

DAVID

Then David said to the Philistine, "You come to me with a sword and spears. But I come to you in the name of the Lord of All, the God of the armies of Israel, Whom you have stood against."
1 SAMUEL 17:45

David was just a boy when he became a great warrior. He was visiting his brothers who were fighting against an army of Philistines when he heard a giant, Goliath, insulting the Lord God. The army of Israel was afraid to fight the giant, but not David. David knew he had God's power with him. He gathered five smooth stones and his sling and met Goliath on the battlefield. David flung the stone and it killed Goliath.

David became famous among the people for his wisdom and great skill as a warrior. King Saul became jealous of him and wanted to kill him, but God protected David. David would be the king God chose to lead His people! Even though he made some bad choices in life, David would always ask the Lord to forgive him. That's why he is called "a man after God's own heart."

LEARN MORE: 1 Samuel 17

ELIJAH

*Then the woman said to Elijah, "Now I know
that you are a man of God. Now I know that the
word of the Lord in your mouth is truth."*
1 KINGS 17:24

King Ahab was an evil king who worshipped a false god
and did things that were wrong in God's sight. Elijah was
a prophet of the one true God. He challenged the fake
prophets of the fake god Baal to a contest. Elijah said
that if God brought down fire upon the altar he built,
then He was the true God. But if Baal brought down
fire to the altar the prophets built, then he was the true
god. The prophets of Baal cried out to their false god all
day and nothing happened. When evening came, Elijah
asked God to bring down fire to prove that He was the
one true God. You know what? God's fire fell on the
altar, burning up the sacrifice and everything around
it! This proved to everyone that God alone was worthy
of worship.

LEARN MORE: 1 Kings 18:20–40

ELISHA

When they had crossed, Elijah said to Elisha,
"Ask what I should do for you before I am taken
from you." And Elisha said, "I ask you, let twice
the share of your spirit be upon me."
2 KINGS 2:9

Elisha was a student of Elijah, the prophet. He learned from Elijah and would go on to do even greater things than Elijah did. Elisha would perform many miracles by the power of God. Why? Because he asked for a double portion of God's spirit when Elijah was taken to heaven.

Elisha sprinkled salt on deadly water and it was made drinkable. He filled enough jars of oil for a widow to pay her debts and for her and her sons to live well. He raised a little boy from the dead. Elisha multiplied twenty loaves of bread into enough food for one hundred men. He healed an army captain of a skin disease. Elisha acted with faith and courage in all he did, and God provided for him.

LEARN MORE: 2 Kings 4

ENOCH

Because Enoch had faith, he was taken up from the earth without dying. He could not be found because God had taken him. The Holy Writings tell how he pleased God before he was taken up.

HEBREWS 11:5

. . . .

Enoch was known as a man who "walked with God." He was 65 years old when he had a son, Methuselah, who would become the oldest known person in the Bible. For three hundred years after Methuselah's birth, Enoch obeyed and served the Lord. Because of his faith, he was taken straight to heaven without dying.

. . . .

LEARN MORE: Genesis 5:21–24

ESAU

The first to come out was red and he had hair all over his body. They gave him the name of Esau.
GENESIS 25:25

. . . .

Esau and his twin brother, Jacob, were born to Isaac and Rebekah. Esau was a hunter and pleased his father, Isaac, because of the meat he brought to him. Jacob was his mother's favorite because he was gentle and stayed in the tents with her.

One day Jacob tricked Esau into selling him his inheritance for a bowl of stew. This was only the beginning of the problems the two brothers would have with each other. Jacob stole his father's blessing from Esau and it caused Esau to hate him and want to hurt him. They went their own ways, but many years later, Jacob and Esau met and became friends again.

. . . .

LEARN MORE: Genesis 27:1–40

ESTHER

Queen Esther answered, "If I have found favor in your eyes, O king, and if it please the king, I ask that my life and the lives of my people be saved."
ESTHER 7:3

Esther was an orphaned girl who was raised by her cousin, Mordecai. She was a Jew in the land of Persia, ruled by King Ahasuerus. When the king was looking for a new queen, he chose Esther for her beauty and grace. She did not want anyone to find out she was Jewish, because Mordecai told her it might bring her harm.

Several years later, the king's official, Haman, came up with a plot to kill the Jews living in Persia. Then he convinced the king to make it a law. Mordecai found out and told his cousin Esther that she could do something to save her people.

Queen Esther made a bold move that was against the law—she went to the king without being invited. Esther risked her life to save the lives of others. Her courage and bravery spared the Jews in Persia.

LEARN MORE: Esther 4

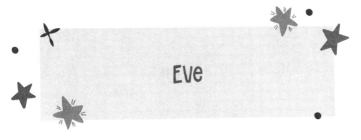

Eve

The Lord God made woman from the bone
which He had taken from the man.
And He brought her to the man.
GENESIS 2:22

. . . .

God created **Adam** as the first man on earth. When God saw that Adam was lonely, the Lord made him fall into a deep sleep. While Adam rested, God took one of the man's ribs and created a woman from it. She would be called Eve, which means "the mother of all living."

God gave Adam and Eve just one rule: they were not to eat from one tree in the garden, the Tree of Knowledge of Good and Evil. God's enemy, Satan, showed up looking like a snake. He told Eve that if she ate of the tree she would be like God. Eve thought that sounded good, so she ate the fruit. Then she shared some with Adam. But that was a **sin** against God and it messed up every human being for all time. Eve's story shows us that even those who walk close to God can be tempted to sin. We must ask God's Holy Spirit to help us overcome temptation.

. . . .

LEARN MORE: Genesis 2–3

GIDEON

The angel of the Lord showed himself to Gideon and said to him, "The Lord is with you, O powerful soldier."
JUDGES 6:12

Gideon was working when the angel of the Lord came to him and called him a "powerful soldier." Gideon didn't feel like a brave warrior. But the angel told Gideon that the Lord had chosen him to save the Israelites from their enemies, the Midianites. Gideon didn't believe he could do the job. But God gave Gideon three miraculous signs, and he agreed to serve as the military leader—or "judge"—of God's people.

God told Gideon to take a tiny army, carrying pitchers, torches, and trumpets, to attack a much larger enemy army at night. At Gideon's signal, they blew their trumpets and filled the camp with noise and light. The enemies were so afraid they started killing each other! Gideon and the Israelites won the victory God had promised.

LEARN MORE: Judges 8:4–28

PEOPLE

GOLIATH

When all the men of Israel saw [Goliath],
they ran away from him and were very much afraid.
1 SAMUEL 17:24

David went to the Israelite army camp to take food to his brothers. The Israelites were fighting against a people called the Philistines. There was a giant soldier on the Philistines' side named Goliath. He bullied Israel's army.

Goliath challenged King Saul to send one warrior to fight him. But not one man volunteered to take on the Philistine champion—not until David stepped up.

Goliath, in full armor with a shield and a sword, stood more than nine feet tall. David was a boy with nothing but a sling in his hand. But the shepherd boy trusted in the Lord. David slung a stone that struck the giant right in his forehead. The Philistine army ran away, but the Israelites chased after them and defeated them.

LEARN MORE: 1 Samuel 17

ISAAC

But God said, "No, but your wife Sarah will give birth to your son. And you will give him the name Isaac. I will make My agreement with him and for his children after him, an agreement that will last forever."
GENESIS 17:19

God promised Abraham that his descendants—his children and their children and their children over many, many years—would become a great nation. The promise began to be fulfilled when Isaac was born to Abraham and Sarah in their old age.

When Isaac was young, the Lord tested Abraham's faith by asking him to offer Isaac as a sacrifice. But just as Abraham raised a knife to take the boy's life, God stopped him and sent a ram for an offering instead.

The Bible describes Isaac as a person who trusted God and lived a quiet life of simple faith (Hebrews 11:17–20).

Isaac was the father of twin sons, Jacob and Esau. Jacob's sons were the leaders of the twelve tribes that became the nation of Israel.

LEARN MORE: Genesis 21:1–8

ISAIAH

This is what Isaiah the son of Amoz saw about Judah and Jerusalem that was coming.

ISAIAH 2:1

Isaiah was chosen to be a prophet to Israel and Judah when God gave the man a vision of Himself. Isaiah saw the Lord seated on His heavenly throne, surrounded by angels and smoke. God asked whom He should send to speak to the people. Isaiah responded, "Here am I. Send me!" (Isaiah 6:8).

Isaiah spoke God's message to several kings of Judah in the capital city of Jerusalem. He warned that the nation would be destroyed by Assyria unless the people stopped worshipping false gods and turned back to the Lord (Isaiah 10:1–10). Isaiah spoke more about the coming Messiah—Jesus—than any other Old Testament prophet.

LEARN MORE: 2 Kings 20

ISHMAEL

Hagar gave birth to Abram's son. And Abram gave his son who was born of Hagar the name Ishmael.
GENESIS 16:15

. . . .

Ishmael was the son of Abraham and Hagar. Hagar was the Egyptian servant of Abraham's wife, Sarah. After Ishmael was born, God spoke again to Abraham. The Lord said that his promise to make Abraham's descendants into a great nation was still true. But Ishmael was not the son to start that nation.

After Isaac was born to Abraham and Sarah, Sarah liked him much better than Ishmael. One day she saw the older boy mocking Isaac, and she became angry. Sarah demanded that Ishmael and his mother be sent out into the wilderness. In this place without food and water, the two almost died, but God saved them. He then promised that Ishmael would also become the father of a great nation. But Isaac's descendants would become the promised nation of Israel.

. . . .

LEARN MORE: Genesis 21:9–21

JACOB

So Jacob gave the place the name of Peniel. For he said,
"I have seen God face to face, and yet I am still alive."
GENESIS 32:30

. . . .

Jacob tricked both his brother and his father into giving him valuable gifts that were not meant for him. Afraid of what his brother, Esau, might do to him, Jacob ran away. One night, he had a dream that angels were going up and down a stairway into heaven. At the top stood God Himself. He promised Jacob that He would fulfill His covenant—His important promise—to him and his descendants.

Later, Jacob had another strange experience—a wrestling match with the Lord. The battle left Jacob with a limp, but God blessed him and gave him the new name *Israel*, meaning "he wrestles with God." Now Jacob was ready to fulfill the purpose God had for his life. Jacob would have twelve sons whose descendants became the twelve tribes of Israel.

. . . .

LEARN MORE: Genesis 32:22–32

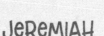

JEREMIAH

*Then the Lord put out His hand and touched
my [Jeremiah's] mouth, and said to me,
"See, I have put My words in your mouth."*
JEREMIAH 1:9

. . . .

Jeremiah was chosen to be God's messenger before he was even born. He was to preach to the people of Judah and tell them that they needed to stop worshipping false gods. They needed to worship only the Lord.

Five different kings ruled during the forty years of Jeremiah's ministry. He was even put into prison for saying that the Babylonians would defeat Judah. Jeremiah's prophecies of disaster were fulfilled during his lifetime. The Babylonian army attacked Jerusalem, tore down its temple and defensive wall, and took its citizens as prisoners back to Babylon.

. . . .

LEARN MORE: Jeremiah 31:31–34

Jesus

*Long ago God spoke to our early fathers in many
different ways. He spoke through the early preachers.
But in these last days He has spoken to us through
His Son. God gave His Son everything. It was
by His Son that God made the world.*
HEBREWS 1:1–2

Jesus was born in a stable in **Bethlehem** while Herod the
Great was king. Jesus was born to a young woman named
Mary. God's Holy Spirit caused her to get pregnant.
Jesus grew up like a regular boy, but He knew what
God the Father had sent Him to do on earth. When
He became a man, Jesus preached and healed, taught
about the **kingdom of God**, and went looking for those
who did not know about God.

Jesus had a ministry on earth that lasted three years—
from the time He was baptized by **John the Baptist** until
He was betrayed by Judas and captured by the Jewish
leaders. Jesus was accused of doing wrong, even though
He had not done anything wrong at all. Jesus was put to
death on a cross. Then He was buried in a tomb, but on the
third day, He rose from the dead! Forty days later, Jesus
went back to **heaven** where He is waiting for the time
that He will return again for all those who follow Him.

LEARN MORE: Colossians 1:12–29

JOHN THE APOSTLE

Going from there, Jesus saw two other brothers. They were James and John, the sons of Zebedee. They were sitting in a boat with their father, mending their nets. Jesus called them.
MATTHEW 4:21

John was one of the first disciples chosen by Jesus. He and his brother James were working on their fishing nets on the Sea of Galilee when Jesus invited them to follow Him and become "fishers of men."

We read about John many times throughout the Gospels, and he called himself "the disciple Jesus loved" in John, the Gospel he wrote.

While He was on the cross, Jesus asked John to take care of His mother, Mary, because the Lord knew He would need to return to heaven. After Jesus left, John worked with the apostle Peter in Jerusalem to tell people about the Gospel. Later, he wrote several books of the New Testament—including the three letters of John and the book of Revelation.

LEARN MORE: Mark 5:37–42

PEOPLE

JOHN THE BAPTIST

John the Baptist preached in the desert.
He preached that people should be baptized
because they were sorry for their sins and had
turned from them. And they would be forgiven.
MARK 1:4

. . . .

When people heard John the Baptist speak, they thought he was a lot like the prophet Elijah from many years before. John lived in the wilderness and told people to stop their sinning. He told them to get baptized to show they were serious about following God. Jesus even began His ministry by asking to be baptized by John.

John the Baptist was later put into prison by King Herod Antipas. John sent his followers to ask Jesus if He was the Messiah, the One that Israel had been waiting for. Jesus reminded John of His preaching and healing in the name of God the Father—that proved Jesus was who He claimed to be. Then Jesus said something very nice: "Of those born of women, there is no one greater than John the Baptist" (Matthew 11:11).

. . . .

LEARN MORE: Mark 1:1–8

35

JONAH

*The Lord sent a big fish to swallow Jonah,
and he was in the stomach of the fish
for three days and three nights.*
JONAH 1:17

God told Jonah to preach to the people of Assyria, an enemy nation that Israel hated. But Jonah did not want to obey God's command. So he got on board a ship that would take him in the opposite direction.

As punishment for his disobedience, the Lord sent a huge fish to swallow Jonah. Jonah was in the belly of the fish for three days and nights. God then had the fish spit him up on dry land. This time, Jonah went directly to Assyria's capital city.

When Jonah preached the message God gave him, the people asked **forgiveness** for their sins and turned to the Lord. That's good news! But Jonah was disappointed that they would not be punished. Jonah was reminded that **God's love** isn't just for certain people—it is for all people and nations of the world.

LEARN MORE: Jonah 4:1–11

JONATHAN

*Jonathan made David promise again,
by his love for him. For he loved
him as he loved his own life.*
1 SAMUEL 20:17

. . . .

Jonathan was the son of King Saul and the best friend of David. Jonathan was first in line to be king after Saul died. But he gave David his royal robe to show support for his best friend. Jonathan realized that God wanted David to be the next king of Israel.

Jonathan even protected David against his own father's anger and spared David's life. Later, when Saul and Jonathan were both killed in battle, David was very sad for his beloved friend. David took Jonathan's disabled son into his home and cared for him for the rest of his life.

. . . .

LEARN MORE: 1 Samuel 20

JOSEPH, SON OF JACOB

"So it was not you who sent me here, but God.
He has made me a father to Pharaoh, and ruler
of all his house, and of all the land of Egypt."
GENESIS 45:8

Joseph was born to Jacob's favorite wife, Rachel. His brothers knew Joseph was their father's favorite and they were jealous of him. They came up with a plan to kill him. His brother, Judah, told them not to kill him but to sell him as a slave instead. After they sold him, they lied to their father, saying Joseph was dead, to cover up what they had done.

In Egypt, Joseph became known for his ability to interpret dreams, including one for Pharaoh, the king. Because of his ability to explain Pharaoh's dream, Joseph was made second-in-command of all Egypt.

Joseph's brothers came to Egypt to buy grain during a famine in their land, and Joseph forgave them for the wrong they did to him. Joseph invited his family to Egypt to escape the famine, saving them from death.

LEARN MORE: Genesis 37

JOSHUA

"No man will be able to stand against you [Joshua] all the days of your life. I will be with you just as I have been with Moses. I will be faithful to you and will not leave you alone."
JOSHUA 1:5

. . . .

Joshua was one of the Israelites who were led out of Egypt by Moses. He was even one of the twelve spies sent into the Promised Land. Only two of the spies, Joshua and Caleb, were confident that they could take the land by God's power.

Joshua became the leader of the Israelites after Moses' death. God told Joshua many times not to be afraid because He would be with him.

The first city that Joshua battled was Jericho. Its thick walls fell after the Israelites marched around the city silently for six days and then blew trumpets and shouted on the seventh day. God was showing His people that they could only enter the Promised Land by His power.

. . . .

LEARN MORE: Joshua 6

JOSIAH

Josiah did what is right in the eyes of the Lord.
He walked in all the way of his father David.
He did not turn aside to the right or to the left.
2 KINGS 22:2

Josiah was only 8 years old when he became the king of Judah. In his first few years on the throne, he probably had trusted advisors to help him lead the country.

Josiah's father had been evil, but Josiah wanted to serve the Lord. He led the nation back to God. He tore down altars to false gods and worked hard to make repairs to God's temple.

During construction, a copy of God's law was found. When Josiah listened to the book being read, he was sad about how the people were not obeying the Lord like they should. Soon after, he asked the people to gather together and promise again to follow the Lord.

LeARN MORe: 2 Kings 22

LAZARUS

*When He [Jesus] had said this, He called
with a loud voice, "Lazarus, come out!"*
JOHN 11:43

Jesus was teaching near Jerusalem when He learned that His friend Lazarus was very sick. Jesus waited two days before going to Bethany, where Lazarus lived with his sisters, Mary and Martha. Jesus often stayed in their home when preaching and healing in and around Jerusalem. When Jesus arrived, Martha met Him with the news that Lazarus had died.

Jesus promised Martha that her brother would live again because He had the power to bring dead people back to life. Then He called Lazarus out of the tomb with three simple words: "Lazarus, come out!" Lazarus came out of the tomb still wearing his burial clothes. This miracle caused many to believe that Jesus was the Son of God.

LEARN MORE: John 11

MARY

The angel said to her, "Mary, do not be afraid. You have found favor with God."
LUKE 1:30

Mary was a teenage girl from the village of Nazareth who was engaged to be married to a carpenter named Joseph. She was shocked when the angel Gabriel told her she would give birth to Jesus, the Son of God. She could hardly believe this since she was not married. How could she have a baby?

The angel told her that it would be a miracle and that God Himself would give her the baby. Mary understood how blessed she was to have been chosen to have this promised baby. She raised Jesus with her husband, Joseph.

Mary would later see Jesus' first miracle at a wedding at Cana as well as His death on the cross.

LEARN MORE: Luke 1:26–38

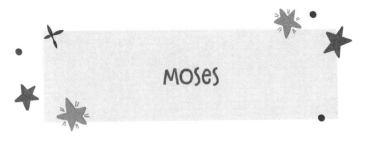

Moses

*Then the Lord said to Moses, "Go to Pharaoh
and say to him, 'The Lord says this: "Let My
people go, so they may worship Me."'"*
EXODUS 8:1

God spoke face to face with Moses "as a man speaks to
his friend" (Exodus 33:11). With the help of his brother,
Aaron, Moses led the Israelites out of slavery in Egypt
and brought them to the border of the Promised Land.

At first, Moses made excuses to try to avoid obeying God. God let Moses know that He would be with
Moses all along the way. Believing God's promise, Moses brought ten plagues against Egypt. These terrible
plagues—things like the river turning to blood and the
death of all of Egypt's firstborn children—finally caused
Pharaoh to let the Israelites go.

Moses then led the people through the wilderness
for more than 40 years. Along the way, God told Moses
how to get food and water, gave him the Ten Commandments (special instructions for the people's behavior),
and helped him build the tabernacle, a place for the
people to worship.

LEARN MORE: Hebrews 11:23–26

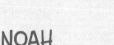

NOAH

And Noah did all that the Lord told him to do.
GENESIS 7:5

Noah was a man who followed God — even in a time when the whole world had become evil. The Lord told Noah that He planned to destroy all living things with a great flood. But Noah and his family would be safe if he would build a giant boat, also called "the ark." Noah obeyed the Lord, built the ark, and entered it with his family and two of every kind of animal. Then it began to rain. The rain lasted 40 days, and water covered the whole earth.

After the flood was over, Noah built an altar and offered a sacrifice of thanksgiving to God. The Lord told Noah that He would never again flood the whole world. He sealed His promise with a rainbow in the sky.

LEARN MORE: Genesis 8

PAUL

He fell to the ground. Then he heard a voice say, "Saul, Saul, why are you working so hard against Me?"
ACTS 9:4

Paul, who was called Saul when he was born, was a Jewish religious leader who punished and sometimes killed Christians shortly after Jesus went back to heaven. When Paul was on a trip to Damascus to hurt more Christians, he had an unexpected meeting with God. This meeting changed Saul's life, as well as his name!

Soon, Paul was a powerful Christian and one of the first missionaries for the Gospel. During his ministry, Paul wrote 13 letters that are part of our Bible today. They were meant to encourage the churches he founded as well as the people who served with him in his missionary work. These letters—Romans, 1 and 2 Corinthians, Galatians, Ephesians, Philippians, Colossians, 1 and 2 Thessalonians, 1 and 2 Timothy, Titus, and Philemon—make up about one-fourth of the New Testament!

LeARN MORe: Acts 9:1–31

PETER

Simon Peter said, "You are the Christ,
the Son of the living God."
MATTHEW 16:16

. . . .

Peter and his brother, Andrew, were two of the twelve disciples who stayed with Jesus through His three-year ministry. Peter was the first disciple to recognize Jesus as the Messiah—God's chosen One—and understand the reason He came to earth.

Peter promised he would always be faithful to Jesus. But then on the night Jesus was arrested, Peter said three times that he didn't even *know* Him! Jesus forgave Peter, and he became bold in telling others about Jesus. On the day of Pentecost, when God sent His Spirit to live in believers, Peter preached a famous sermon that caused 3,000 people to follow Jesus (Acts 2:14–41). In his later years, Peter wrote the New Testament books of 1 and 2 Peter.

. . . .

LEARN MORE: Matthew 14:24–33

RUTH

But Ruth said, "Do not beg me to leave you or turn away from following you. I will go where you go. I will live where you live. Your people will be my people. And your God will be my God."
RUTH 1:16

. . . .

Because of a famine in **Bethlehem**, a Jewish family—Naomi, her husband, and her two sons—moved to the country of Moab. Her sons married women from there. But while they were in Moab, Naomi's husband and sons died. Naomi and the two younger women were left without any male relatives to help them.

One of Naomi's daughters-in-law was Ruth. When Naomi decided to return to Bethlehem, Ruth wanted to go with her, even though that meant leaving her own relatives behind.

In Bethlehem, because they needed food, Ruth went to the fields to gather grain left behind by harvesters. She met the landowner, **Boaz**, who was a distant relative of Naomi.

Naomi encouraged Ruth become friends with Boaz. Soon, Boaz and Ruth married, and Ruth gave birth to a son named Obed, who would be the grandfather of King David.

. . . .

LEARN MORE: Ruth 1–4

SAMSON

*Then the woman gave birth to a son and
named him Samson. The child grew up
and the Lord brought good to him.*
JUDGES 13:24

Samson was promised for service to the Lord even before
he was born. An angel told his mother that he was to be
a Nazirite—a person who would not drink strong drinks
or cut his hair. As he grew up, he was set apart for the
Lord to use to help His people.

Samson was the last of the judges (or "deliverers")
of Israel and was a great warrior against the Philistines.
God gave him incredible strength to defeat their armies.
But Samson let himself be tricked by a Philistine woman
who found out the secret to his strength—his promise to
God. She had someone cut his hair while he slept, and
he became weak. The Philistines captured Samson and
laughed at him. But God allowed him one final moment
of strength. Samson knocked down a Philistine temple,
killing himself and many of his enemies.

LeARN MORe: Judges 16:28–31

SAMUEL

Then the Lord came and stood and called as He did the other times, "Samuel! Samuel!" And Samuel said, "Speak, for Your servant is listening."
1 SAMUEL 3:10

· ·

The prophet Samuel was born in answer to the prayer of his mother, Hannah, who had not been able to have children. To show her thanks to the Lord, she promised that she would give Samuel back to God's service. Hannah took little Samuel to live with Eli, the high priest of Israel.

Samuel obeyed the Lord, and he was faithful to tell God's message to others. God told Samuel to anoint— pour oil over the head of—Saul, showing him to be the Lord's choice as the first king of Israel. When Saul disobeyed the Lord, Samuel anointed a new king from the sons of Jesse. God made it clear to Samuel that David, the youngest son of the family, was His choice as Saul's replacement.

Samuel appears in the New Testament's list of heroes of the faith (Hebrews 11:32).

· ·

LEARN MORE: 1 Samuel 3

SARAH

*But God said, "No, but your wife Sarah will give birth
to your son. And you will give him the name Isaac. I
will make My agreement with him and for his children after him, an agreement that will last forever."*
GENESIS 17:19

. . . .

Abraham's wife, Sarah, was not able to have children.
That's why Abraham and Sarah were confused when
God promised that they would have grandchildren, and
great-grandchildren, and a future family that were as
many as the stars in the sky. Sarah doubted God's promise. . .but when God says He'll do something, He will.

When Sarah was 90, she and Abraham finally had
their promised son. They called him Isaac, a name meaning "laughter," because Sarah had laughed when the Lord
told her she would have a son in her old age (Genesis
18:11–15).

. . . .

LEARN MORE: Genesis 17:15–21

SAUL

*Samuel said to all the people, "Do you see him
[Saul] whom the Lord has chosen? For sure there
is no one like him among all the people." So all the
people called out and said, "Long live the king!"*
1 SAMUEL 10:24

. . . .

Saul was anointed as the first king of Israel. He seemed
like the best choice when he was anointed by Samuel
before the people. He was tall, strong, and a good warrior.
The people had asked God for a king to rule over them,
and they believed that Saul would be the one to help
them defeat the armies of Canaan.

Saul was a good leader for a short time. But then he
began to make choices that went against what the Lord
wanted him to do. Saul's disobedience caused God to
turn against him. God told the prophet Samuel to anoint
David to be king of Israel instead. Saul's jealousy of David
and his bad attitude toward God caused him to be killed
in a battle with the Philistines.

. . . .

LEARN MORE: 1 Samuel 10

SOLOMON

"So give Your servant [Solomon] an understanding heart to judge Your people and know the difference between good and bad. For who is able to judge Your many people?"
1 KINGS 3:9

. . . .

Solomon was the son of King David and Bathsheba. He wasn't David's oldest son, so he should not have been the one to be crowned the next king. But God had chosen Solomon to reign after David. Solomon asked the Lord not for money or power or fame, but for wisdom to rule the people well.

Solomon's leadership and trade deals made both his kingdom and himself rich. He wrote down many wise sayings in the book of Proverbs. Sadly, Solomon foolishly married many women—around 700 of them! They turned his heart away from God. Some people think Solomon wrote the book of Ecclesiastes late in life, when he had returned to obeying God.

. . . .

LEARN MORE: 1 Kings 3

STEPHEN

*He was filled with the Holy Spirit. As he looked up
to heaven, he saw the shining-greatness of God
and Jesus standing at the right side of God.*
ACTS 7:55

. . . .

Stephen was a follower of Jesus in the early church in
Jerusalem. There were people who believed in Jesus
who did not have enough to eat, and it was Stephen's
job to make sure they received the food they needed
(Acts 6:1–7).

Stephen accused the Jewish religious leaders of
being the ones who killed Jesus the Messiah. He said
they were just like their ancestors, who had murdered
God's prophets in Old Testament times. When he
said that he had seen a vision of God in heaven, with
Jesus at His side, the Jewish leaders became so angry
that they killed him.

The punishment of Christians increased, so many who
believed in Jesus left Jerusalem for safety. As they went
to different areas, they took the Gospel to parts of the
world where people had not yet heard the Good News.

. . . .

LEARN MORE: Acts 6:8–7:60

THOMAS

*Jesus said to him, "Thomas, because you have
seen Me, you believe. Those are happy who
have never seen Me and yet believe!"*
JOHN 20:29

All twelve of Jesus' disciples had a hard time believing
He had been raised from the dead. But Thomas was the
biggest doubter of all.

Thomas was not with the rest of the group when
Jesus appeared to them on the day of His resurrection.
The others told Thomas they had seen Him alive, but
he was not convinced. He told the others that he would
not believe that Jesus was alive unless he could see the
nail marks in His hands.

Eight days later, Jesus appeared again to His disciples. He invited Thomas to touch His wounds. This time
Thomas believed and gladly said that Jesus was his Lord
and Master.

LEARN MORE: John 20:24–31

ZACCHEUS

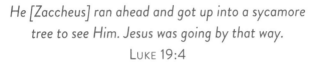

He [Zaccheus] ran ahead and got up into a sycamore tree to see Him. Jesus was going by that way.
LUKE 19:4

Zaccheus was a Jewish man who worked for the Roman government as a tax collector. He cheated other Jews and kept the money for himself. One day as Jesus passed through Jericho on His way to Jerusalem, Zaccheus wanted to get a look at Him. Since Zaccheus was not tall enough, he climbed a tree to get a better view. The tax collector must have been shocked when Jesus called to him by name. Then Jesus invited Himself to Zaccheus's house for a visit!

As he talked with Jesus, Zaccheus realized that he needed to repent for the things he had done wrong. He wanted to make things right again, so he promised to pay people back four times as much as he had taken from them!

LEARN MORE: Luke 19:1–10

PEOPLE

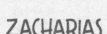

ZACHARIAS

*The angel said to him, "Zacharias, do not be afraid.
Your prayer has been heard. Your wife Elizabeth will
give birth to a son. You are to name him John."*
LUKE 1:13

Zacharias was a priest in the temple in Jerusalem. He and his wife, Elizabeth, were not able to have children . . .and they were getting old.

While Zacharias was doing his job in the temple, an angel told him that Elizabeth would give birth to a son. They should call him John, a name meaning "God has been gracious."

Because Zacharias did not believe the angel's message, he lost his ability to speak until John was born. After his voice returned, he praised the Lord for sending this son who would prepare the way for the coming Messiah. Zacharias's son grew up to be known as John the Baptist, the one who announced the arrival of Jesus the Messiah.

LEARN MORE: Luke 1:5–25

ANTIOCH

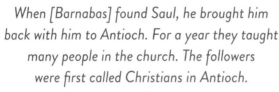

*When [Barnabas] found Saul, he brought him
back with him to Antioch. For a year they taught
many people in the church. The followers
were first called Christians in Antioch.*
ACTS 11:26

. . . .

Antioch was a city about 300 miles north of Jerusalem.
It was one of the largest cities in the Roman Empire
during New Testament times. After Stephen was put to
death in Jerusalem for sharing his belief that Jesus was
the Messiah, many believers left for Antioch.

The church in Antioch became larger, with both Jews
and Gentiles. It was led by Barnabas and Paul, and it is
where the name "Christian" was first used to describe
those who followed Jesus.

. . . .

LEARN MORE: Acts 11:19–26

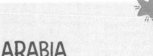

ARABIA

"Some are also men of the countries of Crete and Arabia. They are speaking of the powerful works of God to all of us in our own language!"
ACTS 2:11

. . . .

Arabia is mentioned several times in the Old and New Testaments. Arabia was a desert region outside of Canaan. When the Israelites were taken as captives, the Arabians made Canaan their land and settled in it. Later, when the Israelites returned to their land to rebuild the walls and the temple, the Arabians did not want to give up the land. They considered it their own.

In 1 Kings 10, we read about the queen of Sheba, a famous Arabian who was impressed with King Solomon and brought him many gifts. Solomon and other Israelite kings had traded many items with Arabia.

. . . .

LEARN MORE: 2 Chronicles 9:14

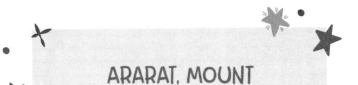

ARARAT, MOUNT

And in the seventh month,
on the seventeenth day of the month,
the large boat came to rest on Mount Ararat.
GENESIS 8:4

After the Great Flood that destroyed the whole world, Noah's ark came to rest on a mountain. There is a mountain range and a specific mountain peak called Ararat.

Today, we do not know for sure where Noah's ark landed. Some believe it was where the countries of Armenia, Turkey, and Iran all come together. The Tigris and Euphrates rivers have their start in this area. Some searches have tried to locate Noah's ark, but it has not been found yet.

ASIA

This is John writing to the seven churches in the country of Asia. May you have loving-favor and peace from God Who was and Who is and Who is to come. May you have loving-favor and peace from the seven Spirits who are before His throne.

REVELATION 1:4

. . . .

John the apostle, Peter, and Paul all wrote to the churches in Asia. But this was not Asia as we think of it today, as the continent containing China and India. "Asia" was a Roman province north of **Greece**. In Acts, we read that Paul spent two years in Ephesus, the capital city of Asia, teaching in a Jewish place of worship. Because of Paul's work there, we see that "all the Jews and the Greeks in the countries of Asia heard the Word of the Lord" (Acts 19:10). All of the Jews and Greeks heard about **Jesus** because of Paul's missionary journey there!

. . . .

LEARN MORE: Acts 19:8–10

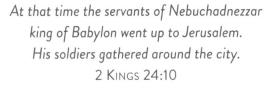
BABYLON

*At that time the servants of Nebuchadnezzar
king of Babylon went up to Jerusalem.
His soldiers gathered around the city.*
2 Kings 24:10

. . . .

The prophet Jeremiah warned God's people that Babylon would take them as captives if they did not stop worshipping false gods. In 587 BC (that means about 587 years before Jesus was born), the Babylonians did capture Judah and took the people as prisoners.

The Babylonians became very powerful when King Nebuchadnezzar ruled. They defeated many nations around them. Ezra 5:14 says, "Nebuchadnezzar had taken the gold and silver objects of the house of God from the house in Jerusalem, and brought them to the house of worship at Babylon." About 50 years later, God allowed the Persian empire to take over Babylon.

. . . .

LEARN MORE: Ezra 5:12–17

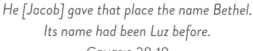

BeTHeL

He [Jacob] gave that place the name Bethel.
Its name had been Luz before.
GENESIS 28:19

. . . .

Bethel means "house of God." It was given this name by Abraham's grandson, Jacob, after he had a vision there. In his dream, Jacob saw angels going up and down stairs to heaven and the Lord was standing at the top. In this vision, God reminded Jacob of the covenant (or promise) He made with Abraham. God said that Abraham, through Jacob, would have many descendants and that they would inherit the land of Canaan.

When Jacob woke up, he made the stone he'd been using as a pillow into an altar and worshipped God. He poured oil over the stone to anoint it and named the place Bethel.

. . . .

LeARN MORe: Genesis 35:1–7

BETHESDA, POOL OF

In Jerusalem there is a pool with five porches called Bethesda near the sheep gate.
JOHN 5:2

Jesus was in Jerusalem to observe a Jewish holy day when He noticed several sick and disabled people gathered around a pool, the Pool of Bethesda. The people believed an angel came every once in a while to stir the waters, and whoever entered the pool first would be healed.

Although he tried, one man in the group could not get into the water first because his legs did not work properly. Jesus had compassion on the man and healed him with the command "Get up! Pick up your bed and walk" (John 5:8). Because of Jesus' words, the man was healed instantly.

LEARN MORE: John 5:1–15

BETHLEHEM

"Bethlehem Ephrathah, you are too little to be among the family groups of Judah. But from you One will come who will rule for Me in Israel. His coming was planned long ago, from the beginning."
MICAH 5:2

Bethlehem is a city that is mentioned many times in both the Old and New Testaments. It was the place that Naomi brought Ruth to after leaving Moab. It is where David tended his sheep in the years before he became king. Hundreds of years before Jesus was born, Micah prophesied that the Messiah would come out of Bethlehem.

That prophecy came true when Caesar Augustus told all the people to return to their hometown to be taxed. Joseph and Mary returned to Bethlehem, and Jesus was born there.

LEARN MORE: Matthew 2:1

BETHPHAGE

Jesus and His followers were near Jerusalem at the Mount of Olives. They were in the towns of Bethphage and Bethany. Jesus sent two of His followers on ahead.
MARK 11:1

PLACES

• •

Jesus sent two of His disciples into the village of Bethphage to find a donkey so that He could ride it into Jerusalem. We don't know for sure exactly where Bethphage was, but it might have been on the Mount of Olives, near the town of Bethany.

When Jesus rode into Jerusalem on a donkey, He fulfilled a prophecy of Zechariah from many centuries before: "See, your King is coming to you. He is fair and good and has the power to save. He is not proud and sits on a donkey, on the son of a female donkey" (Zechariah 9:9).

• •

LEARN MORE: Luke 19:29

CALVARY

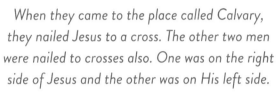

When they came to the place called Calvary,
they nailed Jesus to a cross. The other two men
were nailed to crosses also. One was on the right
side of Jesus and the other was on His left side.
LUKE 23:33

Calvary is a hill just outside the walls of **Jerusalem** where **Jesus** was crucified. The word comes from a Latin word meaning "skull," which is why it is called "the Place of the Skull" in John 19:17. The Aramaic word for this place is *Golgotha* (Mark 15:22).

Jesus carried His own cross partway to Calvary. But He was so weak from being mistreated that the Roman soldiers made a man named Simon help Jesus. Simon carried the cross the rest of the way to the place where Jesus died. He gave His life at Calvary so that we can be forgiven of our sins.

LEARN MORE: Matthew 27:33

CANAAN

*"Send men to spy out the land of Canaan which
I am going to give to the people of Israel. Send
a man from each of their fathers' families,
every one a leader among them."*
NUMBERS 13:2

. . . .

The land of Canaan is also known as the "Promised Land."
It was the land the Lord God promised to Abraham, Isaac,
and Jacob. After many, many years, the Israelites finally
got to move into the land.

Even though Canaan was a small place, it was part of
an important road between Mesopotamia in the north
and Egypt to the south. It had a lot of fruit trees and
vines, and everything grew well there. The men who
had been sent to spy out the area came back and said,
"it does flow with milk and honey" (Numbers 13:27).

. . . .

LEARN MORE: Numbers 13

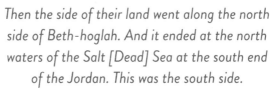

DEAD SEA

*Then the side of their land went along the north
side of Beth-hoglah. And it ended at the north
waters of the Salt [Dead] Sea at the south end
of the Jordan. This was the south side.*
JOSHUA 18:19

The name "Dead Sea" appears only once in the New Life Version of the Bible that we use in this book. It is called the "Salt Sea" in most cases because of the high level of salt found in its water. After the Israelites entered Canaan, this body of water was considered their southern boundary.

The Dead Sea is the Earth's lowest point on land. Its water comes from the Jordan River, but the water does not run out of the sea—it evaporates. The salts and minerals have made its waters almost ten times saltier than regular seawater, and it is a place where no living thing larger than algae can survive. Because there is not much that can live in it, it is known as the Dead Sea.

LEARN MORE: Joshua 3:16

DOTHAN

And the man said, "They have moved from here. For I heard them say, 'Let us go to Dothan.'" So Joseph followed his brothers and found them at Dothan.
GENESIS 37:17

. . . .

Dothan is mentioned twice in the Old Testament. The first time it appears in the Bible, it is the place where Joseph, son of Jacob, met his older brothers as they were watching over their sheep. But before Joseph arrived, they had come up with the plan to sell him as a slave and then tell their father he had died.

The second time we read about Dothan is in 2 Kings 6. Some soldiers were sent to capture the prophet Elisha, but God protected him by causing the soldiers to become blind. When they could see again, Elisha was kind to them. He served the soldiers a meal, even though they had intended to hurt him.

. . . .

LeARN MORe: 2 Kings 6:8–23

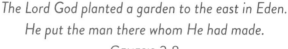

EDEN

The Lord God planted a garden to the east in Eden.
He put the man there whom He had made.
GENESIS 2:8

God created the Garden of Eden as a beautiful place where Adam and Eve could enjoy creation and walks with the Lord. The Garden was filled with many beautiful plants and animals. It was a perfect place to be with God and everything He had created.

On a map today, Eden would be somewhere in the region of Mesopotamia near the Tigris and Euphrates rivers. We cannot be sure exactly where it was located, because Adam and Eve were sent out of the Garden after they disobeyed the Lord. The word *Eden* is sometimes used to describe a place of perfection. When God and His people live together again in eternity, it will be Eden!

LEARN MORE: Genesis 2:4–17

GETHSEMANE

*Jesus came with them to a place
called Gethsemane. He said to them,
"You sit here while I go over there to pray."*
MATTHEW 26:36

The Garden of Gethsemane is where Jesus prayed on the night before He was arrested and then crucified. He took His three closest disciples and asked them to pray for Him. Then Jesus went off alone to ask God the Father if there was any way He could avoid what was going to happen. He knew that He would need to face death on the cross to save people from their sins, but the thought of the suffering and death was difficult.

This garden, on the Mount of Olives, is where Jesus prayed for strength to do what He knew He had to do. In Gethsemane, Jesus told His Father that He would do whatever He wanted Him to do. Because of Jesus' sacrifice, we can each have a relationship with Him simply by asking.

LEARN MORE: Matthew 26:36–46

GReece

*As he went through those parts of the country,
he spoke words of comfort and help to the Christians. Then he went on to the country of Greece.*
ACTS 20:2

. . . .

Greece was a powerful, important place in both the Old
and New Testaments. The apostle Paul wrote letters
to the early Christian churches in the Greek cities of
Corinth and Thessalonica.

A man named Alexander the Great conquered much
of the world before Paul was born, and he brought Greek
culture, customs, and languages to the area around the
Mediterranean Sea. Greek became a common language
during this time. Paul was able to speak Greek to preach
the Gospel of Jesus Christ everywhere he traveled in
his missionary journeys.

. . . .

LeARN MORe: 1 Thessalonians 1

ISRAEL

*"Let us thank the Lord God of Israel. He has
bought His people and made them free."*
LUKE 1:68

God's people were known as the Israelites, getting their
name from their ancestor, Jacob. God gave Jacob the
new name of *Israel* because he wrestled with God and
men and won.

The nation of Israel divided in two after King Solomon died. Ten tribes in the north were still known as
Israel and the two tribes in the south were called Judah.
Both Israel and Judah had their own kings. Sadly, Israel
had many evil kings who worshipped false gods and led
the people away from the one true God. This disobedience and idol worship are the reason that the Israelites
were taken captive by Assyria.

LEARN MORE: Genesis 32:28

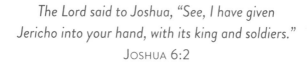

JERICHO

*The Lord said to Joshua, "See, I have given
Jericho into your hand, with its king and soldiers."*
JOSHUA 6:2

Jericho was the first Canaanite city that the Israelites captured. Moses had died and Joshua became the leader of God's people. The last generation of people died out in the wilderness because of their disobedience. Now a new generation was ready to conquer Canaan and move into the Promised Land.

Jericho was a strong city near the Jordan River. It had thick walls and powerful defenses. God told Joshua to lead the people in a silent march around the city of Jericho for six days. On the seventh day, God told the people to march around the city seven times and then to shout and blow their trumpets. When they made this loud noise, the walls of Jericho collapsed. Because of God's power, the city belonged to the Israelites.

LEARN MORE: Joshua 6

JeRUSALeM

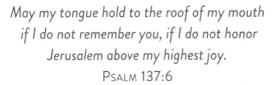

May my tongue hold to the roof of my mouth
if I do not remember you, if I do not honor
Jerusalem above my highest joy.
PSALM 137:6

Jerusalem was a very special city to the people of Israel. It was their most important place from the time of King David through the life of Jesus. It is still an important city today. Jerusalem is often called the "Holy City" because of its importance to both Jews and Christians.

King David made Jerusalem the capital city of Israel. King Solomon built the temple there. And the Israelites rebuilt Jerusalem after they were released from their captivity in Babylon. We read about Jesus going into Jerusalem for holy days, and He was crucified right outside the city. Today, travelers visit sites around Jerusalem where many believe these events happened.

LEARN MORE: Matthew 23:37–39

JORDAN RIVER

*Jesus came to the Jordan River from the
town of Nazareth in the country of
Galilee. He was baptized by John.*
MARK 1:9

The Jordan River runs the whole length of Israel. It starts about 1,500 feet above sea level and flows into the lowest spot on earth, the Dead Sea. This sharp drop is the reason the river was given its name, which means "the descender."

The Jordan River is the place where several miracles in the Old and New Testaments happened. It is where a Syrian army commander named Naaman was healed of his leprosy (2 Kings 5:14) and where God made a path of dry land so the Israelites could cross into the Promised Land (Joshua 3:14–16). In the New Testament, Jesus began His ministry by being baptized in the Jordan River by John the Baptist.

LEARN MORE: Luke 3:21–22

JUDAH

When Rehoboam came to Jerusalem, he gathered all the family of Judah and the family of Benjamin. He gathered together 180,000 chosen men of war to fight against the family of Israel and return the nation to Rehoboam the son of Solomon.
1 KINGS 12:21

. . . .

Judah is the name of the southern part of Israel that became its own nation after splitting away from the north. While the northern tribes kept the name *Israel*, Judah was made up of two tribes that came from Jacob's sons, Judah and Benjamin.

Judah was first ruled by King Solomon's son, Rehoboam. Judah was led by a few good kings and seemed to follow the Lord better than Israel. But Judah also disobeyed God and began to worship idols. The people ignored the messages from God given by prophets like Isaiah and Jeremiah. This disobedience is what caused them to be taken as prisoners by the Babylonians.

. . . .

LEARN MORE: 2 Chronicles 14:2–8

MEDITERRANEAN SEA

*The west side of their land was along the side of
the Great Sea. These are the sides of the land
of the people of Judah by their families.*
JOSHUA 15:12

. . . .

The Great Sea is another name for the Mediterranean
Sea. The Mediterranean Sea is the border on the west
side of the land of Israel. The tribe of Judah owned the
area of land that stretched west to the sea when the
land was divided among the tribes. This happened when
Joshua was their leader.

The Mediterranean Sea stretched from Israel's coast
for about 2,200 miles to the Atlantic Ocean. The Bible
mentions other countries that border the Mediterranean
Sea: Egypt, Syria, Lebanon, Greece, and Italy.

. . . .

LEARN MORE: Joshua 23:4

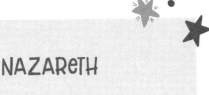

NAZARETH

Jesus came to Nazareth where He had grown up. As He had done before, He went into the Jewish place of worship on the Day of Rest. Then He stood up to read.
LUKE 4:16

Nazareth was a small town where Jesus grew up. Many people thought poorly of Nazareth. A disciple of Jesus, Philip, once invited a friend to come to see Jesus of Nazareth, the Messiah. Nathanael responded, "Can anything good come out of the town of Nazareth?" (John 1:46).

Even though it was just a small, unpopular village during Jesus' time, Nazareth has grown to be the largest city in Israel's northern district. Christians travel from all over the world to visit Nazareth, to see the city where Jesus grew up.

LEARN MORE: Mark 6:1–6

NILE RIVER

"The Nile will be full of frogs. They will come up and go in your house and in your room and on your bed. They will come in the houses of your servants and on your people. They will come in your stoves and in your bread dough."
EXODUS 8:3

. . . .

The Nile River is the longest river in Africa and the second-longest river in the world. It gets its water from different sources in East Africa and empties into the Mediterranean Sea.

Most of the references to the Nile are found in the book of Exodus. The Nile is where **Moses'** mother hid him in a basket to save his life. When Moses was an adult, he proved to Pharaoh that the one true **God** was more powerful than his Egyptian gods through the plagues that God sent. Several of these plagues took place around the Nile, like the time huge numbers of frogs appeared. The Egyptians worshipped the river for the way it gave life. But they didn't realize it was the **almighty God** who created the Nile and provided the water for them.

. . . .

LEARN MORE: Exodus 7:14–25

NINEVEH

*"Get up and go to the large city of Nineveh,
and preach against it. For their sin
has come up before Me."*
JONAH 1:2

Nineveh was the capital city of Assyria. God told the prophet Jonah to warn the Ninevites of His coming judgment. But Jonah traveled in the opposite direction, getting on a boat in the Mediterranean Sea. These people of Nineveh were enemies of the Israelites and were known for being evil and violent. So Jonah was afraid to go anywhere near Nineveh.

After being swallowed and spit out by a giant fish, Jonah finally obeyed God. He preached a warning message to the city. Amazingly, the people believed Jonah and stopped their wicked behavior. But Jonah was angry that they would not be punished for the evil things they had done, and he asked God why they shouldn't be in trouble. The Lord reminded Jonah that He was a loving God who shows mercy even to people who have been very evil. If they turn to God, He will forgive.

LEARN MORE: Jonah 3:1–10

PATMOS

I, John, am your Christian brother. I have shared with you in suffering because of Jesus Christ. I have also shared with you His holy nation and we have not given up. I was put on the island called Patmos because I preached the Word of God and told about Jesus Christ.
REVELATION 1:9

· ·

John the apostle wrote the book of Revelation on this small island in the Aegean Sea. It lies off the coast of what is now Turkey. John was sent there as punishment for sharing the Gospel of Jesus Christ.

Patmos is very rough and rocky. It was only about ten miles long and six miles wide. God used this place and time to give John visions of the future. He wrote them down in the book of Revelation. This book tells us about the coming of God's perfect kingdom of heaven to the earth.

RED SEA

*So God led the people through the desert to get
to the Red Sea. The people of Israel went
out of the land of Egypt ready for war.*
EXODUS 13:18

. . . .

In the book of Exodus, we read that after ten plagues against Egypt, Pharaoh finally let the Israelites leave Egypt. But they had not gotten very far before Pharaoh changed his mind. He sent his army to capture the people and bring them back again.

God commanded Moses to lift his staff (a kind of walking stick) and when he did, God divided the sea in half. Moses led the people across dry land between two walls of water! When all of the Israelites had made it safely across, God let the water close back in, destroying the Egyptian army.

. . . .

LEARN MORE: Exodus 14

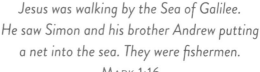

SeA oF GALiLee

Jesus was walking by the Sea of Galilee.
He saw Simon and his brother Andrew putting
a net into the sea. They were fishermen.
MARK 1:16

Many miracles from **Jesus'** ministry take place on or around the Sea of Galilee. It is where He called His first disciples, **Peter** and **Andrew,** to leave their fishing nets and follow Him. It is also where He healed many people who came to Him, and where He fed 5,000 people with one boy's lunch.

On the Sea of Galilee, Jesus calmed a storm that came up while He and His disciples were on a boat. He also walked on water to His disciples' boat and called to Peter to walk on the water too. Peter did fine until he took his eyes off Jesus, then he sank. But Jesus reached out and saved him!

LeARN MORe: John 6:1–27

SINAI, MOUNT

When the Lord had finished speaking with Moses on Mount Sinai, He gave him the two stone writings of the Law, pieces of stone written on by the finger of God.
EXODUS 31:18

. . . .

Mount Sinai is also known in the Bible by another name, Mount Horeb. It is here that **Moses** met with **God**, who spoke through a burning bush. Later, Moses would meet with the Lord again when he received the Ten Commandments, which explained how the people of **Israel** should honor God with their lives.

Sinai is also the place the prophet **Elijah** ran to when he needed a place to escape Queen Jezebel's anger.

. . . .

LEARN MORE: Exodus 24:12–18

TARSHISH

But Jonah ran away from the Lord going toward Tarshish. He went down to Joppa and found a ship which was going to Tarshish. Jonah paid money, and got on the ship to go with them, to get away from the Lord.
JONAH 1:3

The prophet Jonah did not want to obey God's command to preach to the people of Nineveh. So he boarded a ship heading for Tarshish, a city in the opposite direction, several hundred miles away from Israel.

Jonah's journey to Tarshish did not go well. Because of his disobedience, he was tossed overboard in a storm. He was then swallowed by a great fish, but God had the fish spit Jonah up onto dry land. Jonah finally decided to obey and went to Nineveh, where he preached God's message. The people of Nineveh repented because of Jonah's **obedience**, and God did not punish them.

LEARN MORE: 2 Chronicles 9:21

TARSUS

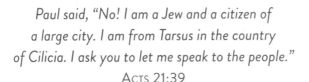

*Paul said, "No! I am a Jew and a citizen of
a large city. I am from Tarsus in the country
of Cilicia. I ask you to let me speak to the people."*
ACTS 21:39

Tarsus is the city where Paul—who was originally called Saul—had lived. He had a job making tents. But he left Tarsus and became one of the Jewish religious leaders in Jerusalem. He punished Christians in Jerusalem because of their love for Jesus. As he was traveling to Damascus to find and hurt more Christians, he was stopped by the Lord.

Paul's life changed immediately. He believed in Jesus as the Son of God. He began preaching the Gospel eagerly.

Paul was worshipping in a synagogue when he was arrested and accused of making the place unholy by allowing the Greeks to enter. Paul stood up for himself by telling the soldiers that he was a Jewish man from an important town: Tarsus.

LEARN MORE: Acts 22:1–23

87

FALL OF SATAN

"How you have fallen from heaven, O shining one, son of the morning! You have been cut down to the earth, you who have made the nations weak!"
ISAIAH 14:12

EVENTS

Before the creation of the earth, we know that there were heavenly beings—angels—who worshipped the Lord. But one of the angels became full of pride and didn't want to worship God. He wanted to be worshipped! This angel was called Lucifer, and he and one-third of the angels were sent away from heaven and the presence of God for their rebellion.

After their "fall" from heaven, they are now known as Satan and his demons.

LEARN MORE: Revelation 12:7–9

CREATION OF MAN

And God made man in His own likeness. In the likeness of God He made him. He made both male and female.
GENESIS 1:27

. . . .

God spent five days creating the universe—the earth and stars, the sun and moon, the birds, fish, and animals. On day six, God created **Adam** to take care of the earth and all that was in it. God wanted other beings to enjoy Him and share in His nature. So He made Adam by taking dust from the ground, forming him, and then breathing His very own life into man.

Adam was made to have a relationship with God and to take care of the earth. God didn't want Adam to be alone on the earth, though, so He created a woman to be Adam's partner. She was given the name **Eve**.

. . . .

LEARN MORE: Genesis 2

EVENTS

TEMPTATION OF EVE

The woman saw that the tree was good for food, and pleasing to the eyes, and could fill the desire of making one wise. So she took of its fruit and ate. She also gave some to her husband, and he ate.

GENESIS 3:6

Adam and **Eve** walked with **God** and enjoyed all of the wonderful things He created. God said they could eat from any tree in the Garden of **Eden** except for one tree, the Tree of Knowledge of Good and **Evil**. One day, as they were in the garden, a snake spoke to Eve and tricked her into thinking that God was keeping a secret from her and Adam.

The snake—who was really Satan—said if Adam and Eve ate from the Tree of Knowledge, they would be like God. The serpent told Eve that God's warning was false—that she wouldn't really die if she disobeyed. So Eve ate the fruit and gave some to Adam, and they immediately knew they had sinned against God. Because of their disobedience, **sin** became a part of the world, ruining their perfect relationship with Him.

LEARN MORE: Genesis 3

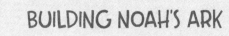

BUILDING NOAH'S ARK

"Make a large boat of gopher wood for yourself. Build rooms in the boat. And cover it inside and out with tar."
GENESIS 6:14

Adam and Eve had sinned many years before. People were born in sin and did many sinful things. God saw how bad everyone had become and He decided to destroy the whole earth.

But God also saw that Noah was still obeying Him. So God told Noah to build a very large boat because a huge rain would soon flood the whole earth. At that time, there had never been any rain before! Noah obeyed God and built the boat, also called the ark. It would be a safe home for him and his family, as well as two of each kind of animal, during the flood.

LEARN MORE: Genesis 6

THE FLOOD

*The flood came upon the earth for forty days.
The water got deeper and raised up the large
boat so that it was lifted above the earth.*
GENESIS 7:17

EVENTS

The ark was built. The supplies were loaded. The animals were on board. Then **Noah** and his family sat inside the ship for seven days, waiting for the end. Their wicked neighbors must have had a good time making fun of them.

At the end of the week, the waters came suddenly. The Bible says that the wells of water under the earth broke open and the windows of heaven were opened. The storm lasted for 40 days and 40 nights.

When the storm stopped and the water dried up, the ark came to rest on **Mount Ararat**. Noah, his family, and all of the animals and birds got off the ark. The people gave thanks to **God** for the way He took care of them.

LEARN MORE: Genesis 8:13–22

BUILDING THE TOWER OF BABEL

So the name of the city was Babel, because there the Lord mixed up the language of the whole earth. The Lord sent the people everywhere over the whole earth.
GENESIS 11:9

After Noah's family left the ark, they began to have children, and the number of people on the earth grew larger. The people all spoke one language and wanted to stay together in one place instead of spreading across the earth as God instructed them. They decided they would build a tower to heaven to make themselves famous.

God saw what they were doing and took away their ability to speak the same language. The people, who were suddenly unable to understand each other, moved out across the land with others who spoke their same new language.

LEARN MORE: Genesis 11:1–9

EVENTS

GOD PROMISES ABRAHAM A SON

But God said, "No, but your wife Sarah will give birth to your son. And you will give him the name Isaac. I will make My agreement with him and for his children after him, an agreement that will last forever."
GENESIS 17:19

Abraham was a godly man who followed wherever the Lord led him. He was disappointed about one thing, though, and that was that he did not have any sons. Abraham and his wife Sarah were very old and had never had children together.

God saw Abraham's faith and told him that he would have a son with Sarah. And God said that Abraham would have so many descendants that they could not be counted. He promised that Sarah would give birth to a son and they would call him Isaac.

LEARN MORE: Genesis 17:17–21

ISAAC IS NEARLY SACRIFICED

The angel of the Lord said, "Do not put out
your hand against the boy. Do nothing to him.
For now I know that you fear God. You have
not kept from Me your son, your only son."
GENESIS 22:12

One day **God** called, "Abraham!"

He replied, "Here I am" (Genesis 22:1). God then told him to take his son **Isaac** and sacrifice him on Mount Moriah. Abraham was stunned. But he trusted in God and set out for the mountain with his promised son.

Abraham was willing to prove his **faith** in God and sacrifice Isaac as God said. Just as Abraham prepared to kill Isaac, though, the angel of the Lord stopped him. God provided a ram—a male sheep—as the sacrifice instead of Isaac. Because of Abraham's faith, God promised that good would come to Abraham and to the whole world through his family.

LEARN MORE: Genesis 22:1–19

JACOB WRESTLES WITH GOD

*And the man said, "Your name will no longer
be Jacob, but Israel. For you have fought
with God and with men, and have won."*
GENESIS 32:28

Jacob had run away from his twin brother, Esau, after tricking Esau out of his inheritance and blessing. He spent many years living in another land. There, he got married and had children, as well as gained much livestock. But after a while, he wanted to return home.

On his journey back to meet his brother, Jacob and a man wrestled all through the night. When Jacob realized that it was not just a man he was wrestling, but God Himself, he said he would not stop wrestling until the "man" blessed him.

God did bless Jacob. And God changed his name to "Israel," which would later be the name of God's special people.

LEARN MORE: Genesis 32:22–32

JOSEPH IS SOLD AS A SLAVE

*Some Midianite traders were passing by. So
the brothers pulled Joseph up out of the hole.
And they sold him to the Ishmaelites for twenty
pieces of silver, and they took Joseph to Egypt.*
GENESIS 37:28

Joseph, son of Jacob, was born to his father's favorite wife, Rachel. Joseph was Jacob's favorite. He got special treatment, including the gift of a colorful coat.

Joseph often told his father when his older brothers were doing wrong. So his brothers hated him. He also told his family the dreams he had about them all bowing down to him. Joseph's brothers came up with a plan to get rid of him.

One day, Joseph was checking up on his brothers, far from their father's camp. The older boys took Joseph's special coat from him and threw him into an empty water pit. Then they sold him to some traveling merchants. The merchants took Joseph to Egypt, where he became a slave.

LEARN MORE: Genesis 37:12–36

EVENTS

JOSEPH BECOMES A LEADER IN EGYPT

Joseph said to them, "Do not the meanings
of dreams belong to God? Tell them to me."
GENESIS 40:8

It was bad enough that **Joseph, son of Jacob,** became a slave in Egypt. Then when someone lied about him, he became a prisoner too!

One night, two other prisoners had dreams, and **God** helped Joseph to explain them. When the king of Egypt, Pharaoh, had some strange dreams, Joseph was called in to interpret them too. He did, telling Pharaoh that the dreams meant a time of famine was coming. Food would be very hard to find unless Egypt saved up food during the good years.

God told Joseph there would be seven years of good harvests before the famine. Pharaoh made an important decision: Joseph would be in charge of Egypt to prepare for the coming disaster!

LEARN MORE: Genesis 41:1–43

THE ISRAELITES MOVE TO EGYPT

"I am God, the God of your father. Do not be afraid to go to Egypt. For I will make you a great nation there."
GENESIS 46:3

The famine that **Joseph, son of Jacob**, had predicted happened in Egypt and nearby countries. Joseph's own brothers, who had sold him into slavery, needed food. When they heard there was plenty of food in Egypt, they traveled there to buy some.

They were shocked and scared to learn that the powerful man selling the food was the little brother they had treated so badly. But Joseph forgave them and told them that **God** had used their bad behavior to save many lives. Joseph sent them back to their home with food. And he urged them to come back to live in Egypt, along with their father, **Jacob**. For years, he thought his favorite son was dead. Now, as a very old man, Jacob would get to see Joseph again!

LEARN MORE: Genesis 46:26–30

EVENTS

EGYPT MAKES THE ISRAELITES INTO SLAVES

A new king came into power over Egypt.
He did not know Joseph.
EXODUS 1:8

EVENTS

Joseph, son of Jacob, was such a wise, good man that Pharaoh trusted him to lead the whole country. Joseph's family was welcomed in Egypt, where they had many babies and grew into a big, strong family.

But after Joseph died, a new king took over. He didn't know Joseph and thought Joseph's family—the Israelites—were a problem. So the new pharaoh decided to make the Israelites into slaves. He put soldiers over them to make them work hard, building cities for Egypt.

The people cried out to God because their lives were so hard. God loved His people and felt sorry for them. So He made a plan to rescue them with a man named Moses.

LEARN MORE: Exodus 1:1–14

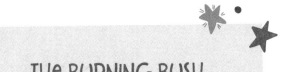

THE BURNING BUSH

There the Angel of the Lord showed Himself
to Moses in a burning fire from inside a bush.
Moses looked and saw that the bush was burning
with fire, but it was not being burned up.
EXODUS 3:2

Moses left Egypt as a young man and then spent 40 years as a shepherd, taking care of his father-in-law's flock. One day, he saw a strange sight: a bush was on fire, but it wasn't burning up! He stepped in for a closer look.

That's when God spoke out of the burning bush and told Moses that He was the God of all and that He had an important job for Moses to do. God wanted Moses to go to Egypt to save His people from their slavery.

Moses had grown up as the grandson of Egypt's king, the pharaoh. But he did not feel important enough to do the job that God was calling him to do. The Lord promised Moses that He would always be with him and would help him.

LEARN MORE: Exodus 3:1–12

TEN PLAGUES ON EGYPT

*"Pharaoh will not listen to you. Then I will lay My
hand on Egypt. By great acts that will punish
the Egyptians, I will bring out My family groups,
My people, the sons of Israel, from the land of Egypt."*
EXODUS 7:4

Moses took his brother Aaron with him to ask Pharaoh
to free the Israelites. God had told Moses that Pharaoh
would not let the people go until he saw God's power.

Moses and Aaron used their staffs (walking sticks)
to bring ten plagues against the Egyptians. "Plagues"
are terrible troubles, things like the Nile River turning
to blood; frogs, lice, and flies covering the land; and the
death of all the Egyptians' cows. Then came a plague of
painful boils on the Egyptians, a hailstorm, a swarm of
locusts that ate all of the Egyptian crops, and darkness
that covered the land. But Pharaoh still refused to let
God's people go. The last plague was that all the firstborn
of the Egyptians families died. Pharaoh's son was one of
those who died, and Pharaoh finally let the Israelites go.

LEARN MORE: Exodus 7:1–11:10

GOD PARTS THE RED SEA

"Lift up your special stick and put out your hand over the sea, and divide it. Then the people of Israel will go through the sea on dry land."
Exodus 14:16

The Israelites thought Pharaoh really wanted them to leave Egypt. But as they came close to the Red Sea, they realized Pharaoh had sent his army to capture them. They couldn't escape because they were trapped by the sea!

But God had a plan. He told Moses to lift his staff, and God sent a strong wind to blow the waters apart. The water turned into walls on both sides of a dry path. The Israelites crossed the sea on dry land. The Egyptians caught up to them and tried to follow them through the sea, but the Lord let the water fall back on them. The whole Egyptian army drowned. The Israelites were safe!

LEARN MORE: Exodus 14

EVENTS

GOD SENDS MANNA

Then the Lord said to Moses, "See,
I will rain bread from heaven for you."
EXODUS 16:4

After the Israelites had traveled in the desert for several weeks, they ran out of food. They complained to Moses, saying that God brought them to the desert to die from hunger. But God promised that He would rain down bread from heaven.

The Lord sent this bread every morning. It was like dew on the grass. The people would gather what they needed for the day. They called the bread manna because that means "what is it?" They ate the manna for 40 years until they came to Canaan, the land God had promised them.

LEARN MORE: Exodus 16:4–36

THE TEN COMMANDMENTS

When the Lord had finished speaking with Moses on Mount Sinai, He gave him the two stone writings of the Law, pieces of stone written on by the finger of God.
EXODUS 31:18

. . . .

God asked Moses to go to Mount Sinai. The Lord spent 40 days there with Moses, giving him the laws for God's people. At the end of the forty days, He gave Moses ten commandments written on stone tablets by His hand. These were laws such as, "Do not have gods other than Me," "Do not make false idols," and "Do not take the Lord's name in vain." The Israelites were also commanded to rest and **worship** God on the Sabbath and to honor their parents, and not to commit murder, steal, lie, break their marriage vows, or covet (to want the things another person has).

. . . .

LEARN MORE: Exodus 20:1–17

EVENTS

TWELVE SPIES REPORT ON CANAAN

Moses sent them to spy out the land of Canaan.
He said to them, "Go up there into the Negev.
Then go up into the hill country."
NUMBERS 13:17

. . . .

EVENTS

When the Israelites came to the edge of the Promised Land, Moses chose one young man from each of the twelve tribes to go into the land. Their job was to find out if they could conquer it.

The men were in Canaan for 40 days. When they returned to Moses, they all reported that the land was beautiful and full of good food. But ten men said they could *not* conquer the land because there were giants living there. Caleb and Joshua were the only two who believed the Lord would give the land to them.

As punishment for Israel's disobedience, God said that none of the people, except Joshua and Caleb, would be allowed to enter the Promised Land.

. . . .

LEARN MORE: Numbers 13:1–14:38

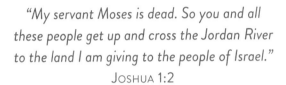

JOSHUA BECOMES THE LEADER

*"My servant Moses is dead. So you and all
these people get up and cross the Jordan River
to the land I am giving to the people of Israel."*
JOSHUA 1:2

. . . .

Joshua was a commander of the Israelite army. When Moses died, Joshua was chosen as the one to lead the people into the Promised Land. God reminded Joshua several times to "be strong and courageous." God knew that Joshua had a big job ahead of him. He had to lead the stubborn Israelites into enemy territory to take over the land of Canaan.

Joshua began to prepare the people to go into the land. He sent spies into the city of Jericho. He knew that he couldn't do anything without God's help, so he sent the religious leaders ahead of them in their march around Jericho as a picture of God going before them into battle.

. . . .

LEARN MORE: Joshua 1:1–11

EVENTS

JeRICHO'S WALLS COLLAPSe

So the people called out and the religious leaders blew the horns. When the people heard the sound of the horns, they called out even louder. And the wall fell to the ground. All the people went straight in and took the city.
JOSHUA 6:20

The people of Jericho were not afraid of the Israelites. They felt safe behind the thick walls of their city. Jericho's residents believed nobody could break through them.

God spoke with Joshua and gave him some strange instructions. For six days Joshua's army, carrying the ark of the covenant, was to walk quietly around Jericho once a day. On the seventh day, they were to walk around the city seven times. When the priests sounded a long blast on the trumpets, the army was to shout. Then the city walls would fall!

It took a lot of faith to believe this plan would work, but Joshua believed. They obeyed God's instructions, and the mighty walls of Jericho came crashing down.

LEARN MORE: Joshua 6

THE DOWNFALL OF SAMSON

Samson said, "Let me die with the Philistines!"
Then he pushed with all his strength so that the
building fell on the leaders and all the people in it.
He killed more at his death than he killed in his life.
JUDGES 16:30

Samson was a judge in Israel who was known for being very strong. God gave him this strength because of Samson's **obedience** in not cutting his hair. Then Samson fell in love with Delilah, who did not obey God. The enemy Philistines had promised her a reward if she would find out the source of Samson's strength. After asking him over and over again, she finally learned that his long hair was the reason he was strong. Delilah called a man to cut off Samson's hair while he slept, and the Philistines captured him. They made Samson blind and forced him to work for them by grinding grain.

During a big feast, the Philistines brought Samson out to make fun of him. But God gave Samson strength one last time. He pushed down the pillars of the temple, causing the roof to fall in and destroy the Philistines inside.

LEARN MORE: Judges 16

SAMUEL ANOINTS DAVID

Then Samuel took the horn of oil and poured the oil on him in front of his brothers. The Spirit of the Lord came upon David with strength from that day on.
1 Samuel 16:13

EVENTS

After the judges, **Israel** wanted a king. The prophet Samuel didn't think that was a good idea, but God told him to anoint a tall, good-looking man named Saul. Before long, King Saul was making choices that went against God. The Lord told the prophet to stop feeling bad about it and go to **Bethlehem**. God had chosen a new king.

A man named Jesse and his sons had come to offer a sacrifice. When Samuel saw Eliab, Jesse's tall, handsome, oldest son, he thought he would make a good king. But God told Samuel, "The Lord does not look at the things man looks at. A man looks at the outside of a person, but the Lord looks at the heart" (1 Samuel 16:7). David was Jesse's youngest son and looked the least like a king. But when he arrived, God told Samuel to anoint him as king.

LEARN MORE: 1 Samuel 16:1–13

110

DAVID AND GOLIATH

So David won the fight against the
Philistine with a sling and a stone.
1 SAMUEL 17:50

The Philistines were in a battle against the Israelites. Goliath, a Philistine giant, marched forward and dared any Israelite soldier to fight him. For 40 days, no Israelite dared step forward.

One day, **David** came to deliver food to his brothers, who were in the army. When he heard Goliath's challenge, he asked for permission to fight, and King **Saul** said yes. David shouted to Goliath, "You come to me with a sword and spears. But I come to you in the name of the Lord of All" (1 Samuel 17:45). David wasn't wearing battle armor but rushed toward the giant fighter anyway. As he ran, he swung his sling and sent a stone slamming into the giant's forehead. Goliath fell to the ground, and David cut his head off! The Philistine army fled, and **God** gave the Israelites a great victory.

LEARN MORE: 1 Samuel 17

SOLOMON PRAYS FOR WISDOM

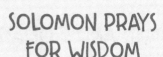

"So give Your servant an understanding heart to judge Your people and know the difference between good and bad. For who is able to judge Your many people?"
1 KINGS 3:9

EVENTS

David was king for 40 years. He made some mistakes, but he was known as "a man after God's own heart." When he was close to dying, David said his son Solomon should be the next king.

As a young man, Solomon loved the Lord and obeyed all His commandments. One night while he was sleeping, God appeared to Solomon in a dream and said, "Ask what you wish Me to give you" (1 Kings 3:5). Solomon could have asked for money or to win every battle. Instead, he asked that he would be a wise king. This answer pleased God.

The Lord gave Solomon what he asked for, making him wiser than any other man on earth. And because he didn't ask for anything selfishly, God also gave Solomon what he had not asked for—great riches, honor, and peace in his kingdom.

LEARN MORE: 1 Kings 3:1–15

ISRAEL DIVIDES

All Israel saw that the king did not listen to them.
So they said to the king, "What share do we have in
David? We have no share in the son of Jesse! To your
tents, O Israel! Now look after your own house,
David!" So Israel went to their tents.
1 KINGS 12:16

EVENTS

King Solomon started well, but then made some terrible choices. He married 700 women, and they caused him to worship false gods.

After Solomon died, Israel gathered to make his son Rehoboam king. But they asked Rehoboam to be easier on them than Solomon had been. He had made them work hard and charged them high taxes.

Rehoboam got some bad advice and told the people he would be even tougher than his father had been. So ten northern tribes broke away to form their own nation. These tribes kept the name Israel, while two southern tribes—Judah and Benjamin—started a new nation called Judah. Israel and Judah would argue and fight against each other for hundreds of years.

LEARN MORE: 1 Kings 11:26–12:24

JONAH RUNS AWAY

*Jonah paid money, and got on the ship to
go with them, to get away from the Lord.*
JONAH 1:3

. . . .

The Assyrians were the most violent and cruel empire the world had ever seen. So at first the prophet Jonah was happy when God told him that its capital city, Nineveh, would be destroyed if they did not repent. But he was scared to go and deliver God's message that they would be punished for their sins. So Jonah took a ship to Tarshish, trying to run away from God.

On the voyage, God sent a storm, the sailors threw Jonah overboard, he was swallowed by a big fish, and was spit up on the shore. Once again he was told to go warn Nineveh, and this time he obeyed.

Jonah was angry that Nineveh had a second chance. He believed they should pay for their sins. But God showed His mercy and did not destroy them, because they stopped their sinful ways.

. . . .

LEARN MORE: Jonah 1–4

ISRAEL AND JUDAH ARE DESTROYED

Then they burned the house of God, and broke down the wall of Jerusalem. They burned all of its buildings built for battles, and destroyed all of its objects of great worth.
2 CHRONICLES 36:19

. . . .

For many years, God's people lived in two nations, Israel and Judah. The kings of Israel were very bad, and led the people to worship false gods. God was very unhappy with this. Even though He warned them through His prophets, the people refused to obey. Finally, as punishment, God allowed the evil Assyrians to overrun Israel.

The kings of Judah were a little better. Some of them followed God and led the people to do the same. But overall Judah had many of the same problems that Israel had. God's prophets urged the people to turn from their sins and follow God with all their hearts. But in time, God allowed the Babylonians to destroy Judah and its capital city of Jerusalem. Many people were taken away as prisoners, forced to live in exile in Babylon.

. . . .

LEARN MORE: 2 Kings 25:1–21

DANIEL IN THE LION'S DEN

Then the king was very pleased and had Daniel taken up out of the hole in the ground. So they took Daniel out of the hole and saw that he had not been hurt at all, because he had trusted in his God.

DANIEL 6:23

Daniel was a young man from Judah taken away into exile. Because he honored God in all he did, Daniel became an important leader in the government of Babylon and Persia. This made many of the other leaders jealous. So they got King Darius to make a law that no one could pray to any god for 30 days—only to the king. Anyone who disobeyed should be thrown in to the lions' den. Darius agreed, and it became law.

Daniel continued praying faithfully to God. When the leaders told King Darius about Daniel breaking the law, the king was sad. But he could not undo the law. Darius had Daniel thrown into the lions' den.

The next morning, the king called to Daniel, asking if he was still alive. Daniel told him yes—God had sent an angel to shut the lions' mouths. He was safe!

LEARN MORE: Daniel 6

Jesus Is Born in Bethlehem

Her first son was born. She put cloth around Him and laid Him in a place where cattle are fed. There was no room for them in the place where people stay for the night.
Luke 2:7

. . . .

Many years after Daniel, the Roman Empire ruled the lands of the Bible. The leader, Caesar Augustus, announced that the entire Roman world would be taxed. Everyone had to return to their family's hometown. A couple named Joseph and Mary, descendants of King David, had to travel to Bethlehem. Mary was pregnant as they made the journey.

When they arrived, the town was full of people who had also come to register. There was no place for them to stay. Mary and Joseph took shelter in a cave that served as an animal stable. That's where Jesus was born.

Shepherds were watching their flocks in the hills nearby. An angel appeared to them, telling them the good news that the Messiah was born. A huge number of angels suddenly appeared, and they were praising God. The shepherds were amazed. They quickly left their flocks and went to find Jesus to worship Him.

. . . .

LEARN MORE: Luke 2:1–20

EVENTS

VISIT OF THE WISE MEN

They [the wise men] went into the house and found the young Child with Mary, His mother. Then they got down before Him and worshiped Him. They opened their bags of riches and gave Him gifts of gold and perfume and spices.
MATTHEW 2:11

Wise men who lived in Persia saw a new, bright star in the skies and were certain it meant a great king had been born in Israel. They traveled to Jerusalem, and when they arrived, they went to King Herod's palace. They asked, "Where is the King of the Jews Who has been born? We have seen His star in the East. We have come to worship Him" (Matthew 2:2).

Herod was worried that this new king would take his power away from him. He told the wise men to go to Bethlehem and search for the child, then come back and tell him where they found Him. The wise men found Jesus, gave Him gifts, and worshipped Him. But they did not go back to King Herod, who really wanted to *kill* Jesus. God had warned them about returning to tell him that they had found the baby king.

LEARN MORE: Matthew 2:1–12

Jesus Amazes The Teachers

Three days later they found Him in the house of God.
He was sitting among the teachers. He was hearing
what they said and asking questions.
Luke 2:46

EVENTS

When **Jesus** was twelve years old, He went with His parents to **Jerusalem** to celebrate Passover. Joseph and **Mary** left the city with a crowd of fellow travelers after Passover, but Jesus stayed at the temple. His parents thought He was with them in the traveling group, but when they realized Jesus was not with them, they hurried back to Jerusalem and searched for Him for three days.

Mary and Joseph finally found Him in the temple, talking with the teachers. "All those who heard Him were surprised and wondered about His understanding and at what He said" (Luke 2:47). People were amazed at Jesus' wisdom, even at a young age. They didn't understand when He told them, "Do you not know that I must be in My Father's house?" (Luke 2:49). He meant His heavenly Father, **God**.

LEARN MORE: Luke 2:41–52

THE DEVIL TEMPTS JESUS

Jesus was led by the Holy Spirit to a desert.
There He was tempted by the devil.
MATTHEW 4:1

After Jesus was baptized by John the Baptist, the Holy Spirit led Him into the desert. Jesus fasted (He did not eat) for forty days. Then the devil tempted Him, saying, "If You are the Son of God, tell these stones to be made into bread" (Matthew 4:3). The devil also tried to get Jesus to do other things He shouldn't. But Jesus always does the right thing, so Satan lost.

The devil wasn't trying to make Jesus doubt that He was God's Son. Jesus knew who He was. Satan was trying to tempt Jesus to use His power for selfish reasons. But that's not why Jesus had come. He had come down from heaven, not to do His own will, but to do the will of the Father who sent Him. Jesus stayed true to His mission, to die on the cross for the sins of all people.

LEARN MORE: Matthew 4:1–11

EVENTS

JeSUS CALLS
FOUR FISHERMEN

Jesus said to them, "Follow Me.
I will make you fish for men!"
MARK 1:17

. . . .

After Jesus was tempted by the devil in the wilderness, He went to the town of Capernaum. There, He began preaching, and people began to follow Him. One day, as He walked by the Sea of Galilee, Jesus saw two brothers, Peter and Andrew. Jesus called out to them and told them to leave their fishing nets to follow Him. They immediately dropped their nets to follow Him.

Jesus then saw James and John the apostle mending nets in their boat with their father. He called out the same invitation to them, "Follow Me. I will make you fish for men!" (Matthew 4:19). James and John left their boat and their dad and became disciples of Jesus too.

. . . .

LEARN MORE: Matthew 4:18–22

EVENTS

JESUS CALMS A STORM

He got up and spoke sharp words to the wind.
He said to the sea, "Be quiet! Be still." At once the
wind stopped blowing. There were no more waves.
MARK 4:39

EVENTS

After a long day of preaching the Good News, Jesus told His disciples to take the boat over to the other side of the Sea of Galilee. While they were heading to the other side, Jesus fell asleep in the back of the boat. As He was sleeping, a big storm came up and the boat began to fill with water.

The disciples were very afraid that the storm would make the boat sink. So they woke Jesus up. He wasn't afraid though. Jesus spoke directly to the wind and the waves and commanded them to be still. The storm obeyed immediately.

Jesus asked His disciples why they were so scared and why they didn't have faith. They didn't understand how the wind and waves obeyed Him. But they would learn over time to have more faith in Jesus.

LEARN MORE Mark 4:35–41

A MIRACLE FEEDS A HUGE CROWD

They all ate and were filled. They picked up twelve baskets full of pieces of bread and fish after the people were finished eating.
MATTHEW 14:20

Jesus heard that John the Baptist had been killed by King Herod. The Lord was sad and wanted to be alone for a while, so He took a boat to get away for some time by Himself. The crowds found out where He was going though and followed Him. Jesus made time for the people and healed the ones who were sick.

The disciples wanted Jesus to send the people back home since nobody had enough food. But Jesus took the only food they could find—five loaves of bread and two fish—blessed it, and broke it into pieces. His disciples passed the food around and it was enough for everyone, 5,000 men plus women and children. There were even twelve baskets left over!

LEARN MORE: Matthew 14:13–21

EVENTS

JESUS WALKS ON WATER

Just before the light of day,
Jesus went to them walking on the water.
MATTHEW 14:25

After feeding a large crowd of people, Jesus sent the disciples away on a boat and went by Himself to a mountain to pray. Alone when evening came, He saw the disciples' boat across the water. It was being tossed around by the waves in a storm.

As the dawn arrived, Jesus walked toward the disciples' boat, on top of the water! The disciples were afraid. They thought Jesus was a ghost. How could a person walk on water?

But Peter bravely asked to join Jesus, and Jesus said, "Come!" Peter walked on the water to Him, but when he took his eyes off Jesus, he quickly sank. Jesus reached out and saved him though. Then they got back into the boat and the storm calmed down. The disciples worshipped Jesus and recognized that He was the Son of God.

LEARN MORE: Matthew 14:22–33

MESSIAH ENTERS JERUSALEM

They said, "Great and honored is the King Who comes in the name of the Lord. There is peace and greatness in the highest heaven."
LUKE 19:38

After about three years of teaching and preaching and **healing** people, **Jesus** went to **Jerusalem** for the last time. Crowds who knew of His many miracles—including raising **Lazarus** from the dead—rushed out to meet Him. Jesus sent two disciples to the village ahead and had them bring back a donkey and her colt. This fulfilled an Old Testament prophecy: "See, your King is coming to you. He is fair and good and has the power to save. He is not proud and sits on a donkey" (Zechariah 9:9).

The crowd spread their coats and branches from the trees on the road for Jesus to ride on. As He entered Jerusalem, the entire city was caught up in the excitement. They thought Jesus would bring a change in the government and get rid of the hated Romans. But Jesus was coming to bring a change to people's hearts.

EVENTS

LEARN MORE: Matthew 21:1–11

125

JESUS IS CRUCIFIED

When they came to the place called Calvary,
they nailed Jesus to a cross. The other two men
were nailed to crosses also. One was on the right
side of Jesus and the other was on His left side.
LUKE 23:33

. . . .

EVENTS

The religious leaders hated Jesus. They knew He was popular with the people, and He often pointed out their selfishness and greed. So they worked together to have him arrested and killed.

They took Jesus to King Herod and then the Roman governor, Pilate. They lied about Jesus because they did not like the miracles He was doing and that He was showing proof that He was the Son of God. Pilate gave the people a choice between letting Jesus or another prisoner free. The people, caught up in the leaders' anger, chose the other prisoner, Barabbas. He was a murderer.

Jesus was sentenced to die on a cross. He carried the cross toward Calvary until He stumbled. Then the soldiers made a man named Simon carry it the rest of the way. Jesus was nailed to the cross and died in pain. Jesus suffered all of this pain in our place so that we can be freed from the punishment for our sin.

. . . .

LEARN MORE: Luke 23:26–49

JESUS RISES FROM THE DEAD

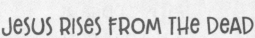

"Do not be afraid. You are looking for Jesus of Nazareth Who was nailed to a cross. He is risen! He is not here! See, here is the place where they laid Him."
MARK 16:6

Jesus had been in the tomb for two days, but on the morning of the third day, the earth shook and an angel of the Lord came down from heaven. He pushed back the stone that blocked the entrance of the tomb. The Roman soldiers guarding it were terrified.

Some of Jesus' friends had come to the tomb to be near His body. But an angel told Mary Magdalene and another woman named Mary that Jesus was no longer there. "He is risen!" the angel said. The women were excited and ran to tell Jesus' other followers. As they were on their way, Jesus met them and proved that He was alive. He told them that they shouldn't be afraid.

LEARN MORE: Matthew 28:1–15

EVENTS

JESUS APPEARS TO HIS DISCIPLES

It was evening of the first day of the week. The followers had gathered together with the doors locked because they were afraid of the Jews. Jesus came and stood among them. He said, "May you have peace."
JOHN 20:19

The disciples had locked the doors to the building they were staying in. They were afraid that the religious leaders who had **Jesus** put to death would come to arrest them too. But all of a sudden, Jesus was standing with them! He told them that they didn't need to be afraid. He had risen just as He'd promised! Jesus showed them the wounds on His hands, feet, and side so that they would believe.

To prove that He wasn't a ghost, Jesus ate some fish. His disciples watched, and they were filled with **joy** when they realized that their Lord was with them again!

LEARN MORE: Luke 24:36–43

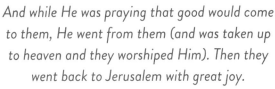

JESUS RISES
UP TO HEAVEN

*And while He was praying that good would come
to them, He went from them (and was taken up
to heaven and they worshiped Him). Then they
went back to Jerusalem with great joy.*
LUKE 24:51–52

EVENTS

Jesus told His disciples to return to Jerusalem. As they
ate together, Jesus commanded them, "Do not leave
Jerusalem. Wait for what the Father has promised. . . .
In a few days you will be baptized with the Holy Spirit"
(Acts 1:4–5).

Jesus then led His disciples out to a place called
Bethany, lifted His hands, and blessed them. At that
moment, He went up into the sky and disappeared
into a cloud. He went straight to heaven where "He sat
down on the right side of God" (Mark 16:19). Then the
disciples worshipped Jesus and went back to Jerusalem,
full of joy.

LEARN MORE: Luke 24:50–53

THE HOLY SPIRIT COMES DOWN

They were all filled with the Holy Spirit. Then they began to speak in other languages which the Holy Spirit made them able to speak.
ACTS 2:4

EVENTS

It was the Feast of Pentecost, and 120 disciples were crowded into the large house of a wealthy disciple. Suddenly the sound of a mighty rushing wind filled the place where they were sitting.

What looked like tongues of fire came from heaven down to each of them. The Holy Spirit filled them inside, and they all began to praise God in other languages.

Jews had come from foreign lands to attend the feast. As the disciples rushed out of the house praising God, people were surprised that they were speaking the same languages that those from foreign lands spoke. Peter explained that this miracle fulfilled a prophecy of Joel in the Old Testament (Joel 2:28–32). Peter told the people that it was time for them to call on the name of the Lord to be saved. About 3000 people made the decision to follow Jesus.

LEARN MORE: Acts 2:1–21

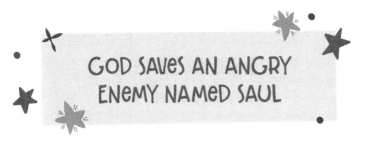

GOD SAVES AN ANGRY ENEMY NAMED SAUL

All at once he saw a light from heaven shining around him. He fell to the ground. Then he heard a voice say, "Saul, Saul, why are you working so hard against Me?"
ACTS 9:3–4

. . . .

Saul was a Jewish leader who hated Jesus and His followers. He was traveling to the city of Damascus to arrest Christians and bring them back to Jerusalem.

But suddenly, a light blazed around him. Saul fell to the ground and heard the voice of Jesus. The Lord told Saul to get up and go into Damascus. Arise, and go into the city, where "you will be told what to do" (verse 6).

Blinded by the light, Saul needed help to get into town. There, God sent a believer named Ananias to pray for Saul. He got his sight back and was filled with the Holy Spirit. Then Saul was baptized, and he quickly began preaching the truth about Jesus!

. . . .

LEARN MORE: Acts 9:1–18

PAUL BECOMES A MISSIONARY

All at once the earth started to shake. The stones under the prison shook and the doors opened. The chains fell off from everyone.
Acts 16:26

Saul, for many years an enemy of Jesus, had gotten saved. Now known as Paul, he traveled around sharing the good news of the Gospel.

In the city of Athens, Greece, Paul was struck by how many idols and pagan temples there were. Towering over Athens was the Acropolis, filled with temples to the Greek gods.

Paul was preaching in the marketplace when some really smart people heard him. He taught how Jesus had risen from the dead, a strange idea to Greeks. So they brought him to Mars Hill to the city's ruling religious leaders.

Paul said he had seen an altar in their city with a message chiseled on the side: TO THE UNKNOWN GOD. Then he said, "You are worshiping Him without knowing Him. He is the One I will tell you about" (Acts 17:23). That "One" was Jesus!

LEARN MORE: Acts 17:16–34

JESUS RETURNS TO EARTH

*See! He is coming in the clouds. Every eye will see Him.
Even the men who killed Him will see Him. All the
people on the earth will cry out in sorrow
because of Him. Yes, let it be so.*
REVELATION 1:7

Why would someone like Paul give his life to tell people about Jesus? Because Jesus is coming back! He will come on the clouds of heaven with power and glory. Then the angels "will gather God's people together from the four winds" (Matthew 24:31).

When he was on an island called Patmos, Jesus' disciple and friend John the apostle had a vision. Jesus was sitting on a cloud, holding a harvesting tool. He then "harvested" the earth, taking all those who believe in Him with Him to heaven (Revelation 14:14–16) .

When we choose to follow Jesus, we can face even the hardest times on earth with hope. We know that He will someday take us to heaven to be with Him.

LEARN MORE: Matthew 24:3–31

EVENTS

HEAVEN COMES TO EARTH

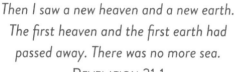

*Then I saw a new heaven and a new earth.
The first heaven and the first earth had
passed away. There was no more sea.*
REVELATION 21:1

At the end of time, God will make the earth new and create new heavens. There will be "no more sea." This probably means that there will be plenty of land for people to live on.

Then the city of light, "New Jerusalem," will come down out of the heavens and settle on earth. God Himself lives in that city, so He will then be living on this beautiful new planet with all those who believe in Him. This will be the beautiful ending to the long history of God's dealings with people. And it will be the beginning of His wonderful forever!

. . . .

LEARN MORE: Revelation 217

134

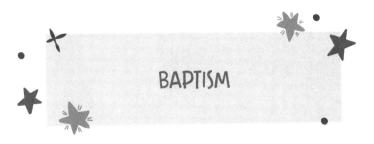

BAPTISM

*When you were baptized, you were buried as Christ
was buried. When you were raised up in baptism,
you were raised as Christ was raised. You were
raised to a new life by putting your trust in God.
It was God Who raised Jesus from the dead.*
COLOSSIANS 2:12

• •

Baptism shows that a person believes in God and has put their faith in Jesus. It was first seen in the ministry of John the Baptist. He told people to repent and be baptized to show their sin was washed away. Jesus asked John to baptize Him at the beginning of His ministry. By doing that, He showed an example for all people who would believe and be baptized in His name.

Christian groups continue to baptize believers of Christ. There are different ways baptism is done, whether by dunking in water or sprinkling. But the purpose of baptism is to remember the death, burial, and resurrection of Jesus Christ. It is a celebration of the new life Jesus gives to those who accept Him as Lord and Savior.

IDEAS

• •

LEARN MORE: Romans 6:4

BLESSING

*When someone does something bad to you,
do not do the same thing to him. When someone
talks about you, do not talk about him. Instead,
pray that good will come to him. You were called to
do this so you might receive good things from God.*
1 PETER 3:9

A blessing is a kindness spoken or shown to another person. God blesses people, and people can also bless each other (Genesis 49:1–28).

In the Old Testament, a blessing carried great power. Once a blessing was spoken, it could not be changed or given to someone else (Genesis 27:30–35). Jacob tricked his father, Isaac, into blessing him instead of his older brother, so Esau did not receive the blessing that was meant for him.

God is the Giver of all blessings, and He wants to bless all people. Since His Son, Jesus, came into the world, His greatest blessing is to those who believe in Christ as their Savior. God blesses His people by forgiving our sins and giving us eternal life.

LEARN MORE: Genesis 12:2

BORN AGAIN

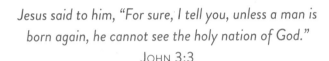

Jesus said to him, "For sure, I tell you, unless a man is born again, he cannot see the holy nation of God."
JOHN 3:3

Being "born again" means becoming a member of God's family—becoming His child. The phrase comes from Jesus' talk with Nicodemus, a religious leader who went to Jesus to ask questions to learn more about Him.

Nicodemus didn't understand the idea. He wondered how a person could be born from his mom a second time. Jesus explained that He was talking about a new birth inside—in a person's spirit.

The apostle Paul described being born again in his letter to Christians in Corinth. "If a man belongs to Christ, he is a new person. The old life is gone. New life has begun" (2 Corinthians 5:17).

When people give Jesus control of their lives instead of themselves, their sins are forgiven, and the Holy Spirit comes to live inside of them.

IDEAS

LEARN MORE: John 3:1–17

CHURCH

*"And I tell you that you are Peter. On this rock
I will build My church. The powers of hell will
not be able to have power over My church."*
MATTHEW 16:18

A church is a group of people who believe in Jesus and gather together for worship (Acts 15:4). "The church" is all those who have ever lived who chose to allow Christ to be their Savior (Ephesians 5:27). The church is supposed to continue the work of Jesus in the world.

It began with the coming of the Holy Spirit on Jesus' followers on the day of Pentecost (Acts 2:1–6).

Toward the end of His life on earth, Jesus told His followers to spread the good news about His life, death, and resurrection throughout the world (Matthew 28:18–20). The book of Acts tells how the Holy Spirit gave the early church power to carry out this command.

LEARN MORE: Colossians 1:18

IDEAS

COMMUNION

When we give thanks for the fruit of the vine at the Lord's supper, are we not sharing in the blood of Christ? The bread we eat at the Lord's supper, are we not sharing in the body of Christ?
1 CORINTHIANS 10:16

On the night before He was arrested and crucified, Jesus ate the Lord's Supper with His disciples. They came to Jesus in Jerusalem to eat a meal together in celebration of the Jewish Passover. Jesus used the things they ate and drank to tell about His coming death on the cross.

He said that the bread and wine they ate and drank together were a reminder of His body that would bleed to save people from sin. He also told them to remember His death whenever they ate this meal in the future.

The Lord's Supper is still celebrated by churches. Some other names it is known by are Holy Communion, the Eucharist, and the Lord's Table.

IDEAS

LEARN MORE: Luke 22:19–20

CONFESSION

*It will not go well for the man who hides
his sins, but he who tells his sins and turns
from them will be given loving-pity.*
PROVERBS 28:13

. . . .

The word *confess* appears many times in the Bible. It means to admit or take responsibility for your sin and to turn to God for forgiveness.

Another kind of confession is telling others about your faith in Jesus. The apostle Paul said it is important to *confess* to others that you are a Christ-follower, telling them that Jesus is Lord of your life. Paul wrote, "If you say with your mouth that Jesus is Lord, and believe in your heart that God raised Him from the dead, you will be saved from the punishment of sin. When we believe in our hearts, we are made right with God. We tell with our mouth how we were saved from the punishment of sin" (Romans 10:9–10).

. . . .

LEARN MORE: James 5:16

IDEAS

COURAGE

*"Be strong and have strength of heart. For you
will bring the people in to take this land which
I promised to their fathers to give them."*
JOSHUA 1:6

. . . .

God spoke these words to Joshua when he became the
leader of the Israelites after Moses died. God promised
Joshua that He would be with him, just as He had done
with Moses. Joshua had courage and led the Israelites to
conquer the Canaanites and make the land their home.

Another example of courage is the prophet Jeremiah.
For years, he warned the people of Judah they would be
overtaken by a foreign nation unless they followed
God. He was made fun of and put in prison. But God
always showed His love to Jeremiah and protected him.

Some people think courage is not being afraid when
there is danger. But a better way to think of courage is
that it is knowing how to control fear. Scary things will
happen, but God gives strength to have peace instead
of fear.

IDEAS

. . . .

LEARN MORE: Deuteronomy 31:6

CREATION

"Our Lord and our God, it is right for You to have the shining-greatness and the honor and the power. You made all things. They were made and have life because You wanted it that way."
REVELATION 4:11

The Bible tells us that God existed before the world began. It was God who created the universe from nothing, simply by speaking. We learn about creation in Genesis 1, which gives details of everything God created in six days. On the sixth day, He made humans and gave them the responsibility of taking care of all of the plants and animals He made in the days before.

God has kept the world and everything in it running in an orderly way. The prophet Jeremiah said, "When He speaks, there is a storm of waters in the heavens. He makes the clouds rise from the ends of the earth. He makes lightning for the rain, and brings out the wind from His store-houses" (Jeremiah 10:13).

LEARN MORE: Genesis 1

IDEAS

CRUCIFIXION

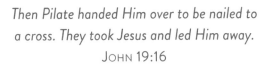

Then Pilate handed Him over to be nailed to
a cross. They took Jesus and led Him away.
JOHN 19:16

. . . .

Crucifixion was a form of punishment that the Roman government used for killing the worst criminals. A person's wrists were nailed to a beam of wood, which was attached to a stake in the ground. Sometimes the person's feet were nailed to the stake. As the person hung on the cross, breathing became very difficult. It was a slow, painful way to die.

In Jesus' time, crucifixion was a dishonorable way to die. But by His sacrifice, Jesus turned the cross into a badge of honor (Philippians 2:5–8).

. . . .

LEARN MORE: John 19:17–37

IDEAS

ETERNITY

But You and Your name, O Lord, will always
be forever and to all people for all time.
PSALM 102:12

. . . .

People are limited by time—we are born on a certain date and we die on another date. This is not true of God. Not only has God existed forever—since before time began—but He will exist for all time to come. He is the eternal One who has no beginning or end.

It's difficult for people to understand eternity because we think of everything in terms of time. To us, a lifetime of 70 or 80 years seems long, but this is no more than the blink of an eye from God's perspective.

The God who lives forever shares the blessing of eternity with those who believe in His Son. "God's free gift is life that lasts forever. It is given to us by our Lord Jesus Christ" (Romans 6:23).

IDEAS

. . . .

LEARN MORE 2 Corinthians 4:18

EVIL

*The eyes of the Lord are in every place,
watching the bad and the good.*
PROVERBS 15:3

. . . .

Sin and evil entered the world when Adam and Eve disobeyed God's command in the Garden of Eden, eating the fruit God had told them to avoid (Genesis 3:6). The sin that began back then is the cause of the evil and suffering in our world today.

God gave the first humans freedom to make their own choices, and He gives us that same freedom. We can choose to love God and follow Him. Or we can choose to follow our sin and selfishness. But that will lead us to a life of trouble and destruction.

Thankfully, we have a loving Father who forgives us of our sinful choices because Jesus died on the cross for those sins.

IDEAS

. . . .

LEARN MORE: Romans 7:7–25

FAITH

Now faith is being sure we will get what we hope for.
It is being sure of what we cannot see.
HEBREWS 11:1

Hebrews 11 is known as the "faith chapter" of the New Testament. The writer begins the chapter with a definition of faith—trust in God, whom we cannot see but who is living and can work in our lives.

Salvation is only possible because of God's grace. But it is not complete without faith—that is, accepting Jesus Christ as Savior and Lord. As the apostle Paul said, "By His loving-favor you have been saved from the punishment of sin through faith. It is not by anything you have done. It is a gift of God" (Ephesians 2:8).

LEARN MORE: Romans 1:17

IDEAS

FORGIVENESS

*You must be kind to each other. Think of the other
person. Forgive other people just as God forgave
you because of Christ's death on the cross.*
EPHESIANS 4:32

. . . .

To be forgiven is to have someone excuse the wrong done
against him or her. Forgiveness among people is possible
because of God's forgiveness of our sin against Him.

Human sin deserves the Lord's punishment because
it goes against His holiness. In Old Testament times, God
accepted an animal sacrifice as a way for people to pay
for their sins and receive His forgiveness. In the New
Testament, when Jesus died on the cross, He became
the sacrifice for the sins of people. He is the reason
anyone can be forgiven by God! Because we have been
forgiven through Jesus' sacrifice, we are expected to be
generous in our forgiveness of others.

IDEAS

. . . .

LEARN MORE: Matthew 18:21–22

GIVING

Each man should give as he has decided in his heart.
He should not give, wishing he could keep it. Or he
should not give if he feels he has to give. God loves
a man who gives because he wants to give.
2 CORINTHIANS 9:7

This verse is part of the apostle Paul's request to the Christians of Corinth to give to an offering for needy believers in Jerusalem. He did not tell them the amount that each believer should give. He wanted the gifts to be whatever a person felt like they wanted to give. Paul wanted the people to give from the right heart—not with a frown on their face or because they were forced into it.

They were to give out of a spirit of love because God's love was shown to us through His Son, Jesus Christ. True love is always giving itself away.

IDEAS

LEARN MORE: Matthew 25:31–46

GOSPEL

I am not ashamed of the Good News. It is the power of God. It is the way He saves men from the punishment of their sins if they put their trust in Him. It is for the Jew first and for all other people also.

ROMANS 1:16

. . . .

The word for *Gospel* in the New Testament means "good news." That's exactly what the Gospel is—the good news that we can be saved from our sins. Why? Because God the Father has offered salvation through His Son, Jesus Christ.

Jesus is more than someone who tells the good news—He *is* the Good News. God's good news to all people was in Jesus' teachings, but it was also in His death and His resurrection.

The good news of the Gospel continues to be powerful in the world today through the work of the Holy Spirit in the church. All believers are called to share this good news with other people.

. . . .

LEARN MORE: Matthew 4:23

IDEAS

GRACE

Then our Lord gave me much of His loving-favor and faith and love which are found in Christ Jesus.
1 TIMOTHY 1:14

Grace is God's favor given to sinful human beings who don't deserve it. The biggest expression of God's grace was the gift of His Son, Jesus, to the world. Christ was the perfect example of grace, bringing it to sinful people so that they could be saved (Titus 2:11).

God's grace is one of the main points in the writings of the apostle Paul. At first, he was unkind and punished the people of the church. But Paul's heart was changed by God's grace, and he became a bold missionary, sharing the Gospel with everyone around him. In all of his writings, he made it clear he thanked God for His grace and for how it can change a person's life.

IDEAS

LEARN MORE: 1 Corinthians 15:9–10

HeALING

Jesus went over all Galilee. He taught in their places of worship and preached the Good News of the holy nation. He healed all kinds of sickness and disease among the people.
MATTHEW 4:23

Jesus came into the world to give humans a way to be saved from sin. But He was also concerned about those who suffered from physical problems. He healed many people during His earthly ministry.

Jesus also gave His disciples the power to heal people (Luke 9:2). They continued after Jesus went back to heaven. Peter and John the apostle healed a lame beggar at the temple in Jerusalem by calling on the name of Jesus and commanding him to "get up and walk" (Acts 3:6).

The book of James gives us a similar command, to lay hands on people and pray for their healing. The Holy Spirit gives us power too, just as Jesus and His disciples had power.

IDEAS

LeARN MORe: James 5:13–18

HeaVeN

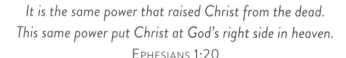

It is the same power that raised Christ from the dead.
This same power put Christ at God's right side in heaven.
EPHESIANS 1:20

Heaven is such a beautiful place that human words cannot describe it. But the words of the Bible writers paint a picture of what heaven is like.

Heaven is a place where we will enjoy fellowship with God for eternity (Revelation 21:3). While heaven itself will be beautiful, our greatest joy will come from being with the Lord.

In heaven, believers will be together again with their relatives and friends who had also chosen to follow Jesus. "Those of us who are still living here on earth will be gathered together with them in the clouds. We will meet the Lord in the sky and be with Him forever" (1 Thessalonians 4:17).

LEARN MORE: Revelation 11:15–19

IDEAS

HOLINESS

For God has not called us to live in sin.
He has called us to live a holy life.
1 THESSALONIANS 4:7

Holiness is one of the qualities of **God**'s character. Throughout the Bible, He reminds His people, "Be holy, for I the Lord your God am holy" (Leviticus 19:2).

To be holy means to be "set apart." God's holiness set Him apart from humans or any other part of His **creation**. He cannot do anything impure, imperfect, or sinful.

Jesus was the perfect example of holiness. It's not possible in this life for weak and sinful human beings to have the level of holiness that belongs to the three persons of the Trinity—Father, Son, and Holy Spirit. But the Bible does say that believers should grow toward this way of life (1 Peter 1:15–16).

LEARN MORE: 1 Peter 2:5

IDEAS

HOPe

Happy is he whose help is the God of Jacob,
and whose hope is in the Lord his God.
PSALM 146:5

Most people think of hope as a feeling that what they want to happen will happen. For believers in Jesus, hope is a strong faith in God's promises. Hope does not come from what we want but from God, who is our reason for hope.

The Bible warns about placing hope in things that are not going to last. These include wealth (Proverbs 11:28), military power (Isaiah 31:1–3), and earthly rulers (Psalm 146:3). Only the Lord should be our hope.

A Christian can put hope in Jesus because He died and rose again to save us. And with hope, we can look forward to His return and His promise of eternity with Him.

LEARN MORE: Hebrews 6:19–20

IDEAS

JEALOUSY

The Jews were filled with jealousy when they saw so many people. They spoke against the things Paul said by saying he was wrong. They also spoke against God.
ACTS 13:45

. . . .

The jealousy in Acts 13 took place in the city of Antioch during Paul's first missionary journey. Paul was preaching in the city synagogue. The large crowd included many Gentiles (non-Jews). This made the Jews so angry that they threw him out of the city.

God used this jealousy to make His Gospel known. Paul knew that many Jews had their beliefs from tradition, but Gentiles were eager to hear about Jesus. From then on, Paul preached mainly to non-Jewish people.

People are confused by the Bible wording that the Lord is a "jealous" God (Exodus 34:14). Since He is holy and perfect, how can a word like *jealous* describe Him? This is just another way of saying that He does not want us to put anything else in the place He should have in our hearts and minds.

IDEAS

. . . .

LEARN MORE: Romans 11:11

JOY

The angel said to them, "Do not be afraid. See! I bring
you good news of great joy which is for all people."
LUKE 2:10

Some people think of joy as feeling happy. But there's an important difference between joy and happiness. A person is happy when everything is going well. We can have joy even when things aren't going well in our lives. It won't change, because our joy comes from knowing Jesus and remembering all of His promises.

The apostle Paul included joy as one of the nine fruits of the spirit (Galatians 5:22–23). Joy is possible for people who love Jesus even when they go through hard times (James 1:2–3). The writer of Psalms says it this way: "You will show me the way of life. Being with You is to be full of joy. In Your right hand there is happiness forever" (Psalm 16:11).

LEARN MORE: Psalm 95:1

KINDNESS

*For sure, You will give me goodness
and loving-kindness all the days of my life.
Then I will live with You in Your house forever.*
PSALM 23:6

Acts of kindness are a way we can show the nature of God. God is always generous and kind toward His people. In the Old Testament, it takes two words—*love* and *kindness*—to tell about this characteristic of the Lord. A writer of psalms said it like this: "Your loving-kindness and Your truth will always keep me safe" (Psalm 40:11).

God the Father showed His perfect kindness when He sent the gift of Jesus to the world. Jesus showed kindness when He paid the penalty for sin by dying on the cross. He actually took our punishment on Himself. All we need to do is accept His salvation as a gift.

The apostle Paul listed kindness as one of the traits of people who follow Jesus (Colossians 3:12).

IDEAS

LEARN MORE: Ephesians 4:32

KINGDOM OF GOD

*He said, "The time has come. The holy
nation of God is near. Be sorry for your sins,
turn from them, and believe the Good News."*
MARK 1:15

. . . .

With these words, Jesus was saying that God's rule of grace in the world had begun. The kingdom of God would be shown through Jesus' miracles, teaching, and death on the cross.

In His parables (teaching stories), Jesus described the kingdom of God. One story, about a man planting seeds, shows that the kingdom will grow in the hearts of some people, while it is rejected by others (Matthew 13:3–8).

The kingdom of God is a real thing, right now, for those who accept Jesus as Savior. But it will not be complete until Jesus returns to earth. Then He will create a new heaven and new earth where Christians will have an eternal relationship with Him.

. . . .

LEARN MORE: Romans 14:17

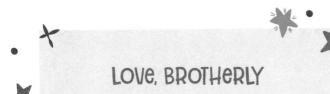

LOVE, BROTHERLY

"I give you a new Law. You are to love each other.
You must love each other as I have loved you."
JOHN 13:34

. . . .

These words of **Jesus** to His disciples are a perfect example of brotherly love, or love for others. Jesus knew their love for one another would have to be strong to help them through the days before and after His death, **resurrection**, and return to **heaven**.

During His time on earth, Jesus said that the second greatest commandment in the law was to love your neighbor as yourself. He gave the Golden Rule as a guide for treating others well. He even told His disciples that they should not hate their enemies but love them instead.

In 1 Corinthians 13, the apostle **Paul**'s "love chapter," true love is described as unselfish and wanting the best for others.

. . . .

LEARN MORE: James 2:8

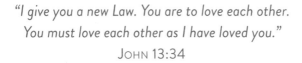

IDEAS

LOVE, GOD'S

But God showed His love to us. While we
were still sinners, Christ died for us.
ROMANS 5:8

. . . .

God showed His love when He saved His people, the Israelites, from slavery, sent them food and water in the wilderness, and gave them a land of their own. Moses reminded the people of God's love when they were getting ready to go into the Promised Land (Deuteronomy 7:7–8).

God's love was shown to all people through Jesus. The greatest way God's love was shown was through Jesus' death on the cross for us. John the apostle wrote, "This is love! It is not that we loved God but that He loved us. For God sent His Son to pay for our sins with His own blood" (1 John 4:10).

. . . .

LEARN MORE: John 3:16

MIRACLE

"How great are the special things He shows us!
How powerful are His wonderful works!"
DANIEL 4:3

A miracle is something that happens that can't be explained by humans. It can only happen because of God and His power.

When Jesus was on earth, He did many miracles. They showed God's power and His love for people. "The blind are made to see. Those who could not walk are walking. Those who have had bad skin diseases are healed. Those who could not hear are hearing. The dead are raised up to life and the Good News is preached to poor people" (Matthew 11:5).

Miracles didn't stop when Jesus went back to heaven. His last words on earth were that those who love Him should keep healing and preaching the Gospel for His glory.

LEARN MORE: Mark 16:15–20

OBEDIENCE

Samuel said, "Is the Lord pleased as much with burnt gifts as He is when He is obeyed? See, it is better to obey than to give gifts."
1 SAMUEL 15:22

King Saul disobeyed God's command to destroy all of the Amalekites' possessions he'd won in battle. When the prophet Samuel asked Saul about it, the king lied. Saul said he planned to offer the animals he'd kept as sacrifices to God. But Samuel told Saul that obedience to God's Word is better than giving a sacrifice to Him.

Obedience is a lot like listening. To hear God's commands is important, but to listen and *do* what He commands is real obedience.

In the New Testament, the apostle Paul wrote about the difference between the obedience of Jesus and the disobedience of Adam. Adam's disobedience brought sin and death into the world. But Jesus' obedience brought God's grace and righteousness to believers (Romans 5:19).

LEARN MORE: 1 Peter 1:13–14

OFFERING

Give to the Lord the honor of His name.
Bring a gift and come into His holy place.
PSALM 96:8

. . . .

An offering brought to the Lord in Old Testament times was placed on the altar by priests. These offerings were certain kinds of animals, wine, grain, or sometimes a complete meal. The sacrifices would cover the people's sins and restore fellowship with God.

When Jesus died on the cross for our sins, the Old Testament way of sacrificing was not needed anymore. The author of the book of Hebrews wrote that Jesus is able to save all people who ask Him to, without a need for an altar offering.

Now the offering that Christians give to God is obedience to His commands.

. . . .

LEARN MORE: Hebrews 10:5–10

IDEAS

PATIENCE

I did not give up waiting for the Lord.
And He turned to me and heard my cry.
PSALM 40:1

Most people think of patience as waiting for something to get better. But in the Bible, God showed that forgiveness was a part of patience. He was patient with His people, the Israelites, when they turned away from Him and didn't do what He asked them to.

The apostle Peter talked about the Lord's patience, using the word *waiting*. He was saying that the Lord is "waiting" for people to turn to Him, because He "does not want any person to be punished forever. He wants all people to be sorry for their sins and turn from them" (2 Peter 3:9).

LEARN MORE: James 5:7

IDEAS

PeACe

The peace of God is much greater than the human mind can understand. This peace will keep your hearts and minds through Christ Jesus.
PHILIPPIANS 4:7

. . . .

After Jesus rose from the dead, Jesus said to His disciples, "May you have peace" (John 20:19). These words were a common greeting used by Jewish people at that time.

When the disciples heard this greeting from Jesus, they may have remembered the promise He had already made to them: "Peace I leave with you. My peace I give to you. I do not give peace to you as the world gives. Do not let your hearts be troubled or afraid" (John 14:27). This let them know that Jesus would be with them through the Holy Spirit, even though He would no longer be there in person.

Since we have been given God's peace, we should live peacefully with all people.

IDEAS

. . . .

LeARN MORe: Ephesians 2:14

PERSEVERANCE

So then, Christian brothers, because of all this,
be strong. Do not allow anyone to change your mind.
Always do your work well for the Lord. You know
that whatever you do for Him will not be wasted.
1 CORINTHIANS 15:58

Perseverance is staying strong, even when things get hard. This is what the apostle Paul wanted for the believers who lived in the city of Corinth. He wanted them to keep following Jesus so they would be witnesses for Him in a city that was famous for its people's bad behavior.

We are only saved because of our faith in Jesus. But perseverance in doing good things shows other people that we have faith. The book of James says, "Faith is dead when nothing is done" (James 2:26).

An example of perseverance is Jesus Himself. The author of Hebrews encouraged his readers to finish the "race" of a Christian life by following Jesus' example.

LEARN MORE: Hebrews 12:1–15

PRAYER

We are sure that if we ask anything that
He wants us to have, He will hear us.
1 JOHN 5:14

. . . .

In this verse, **John the apostle** says that the Lord has promised to hear us when we pray. The apostle **Peter** wrote, "The Lord watches over those who are right with Him. He hears their prayers" (1 Peter 3:12).

Most of us think of prayer as a time when we ask **God** for something. When we request Him to do something for ourselves or others, that is a prayer of "petition." But there is so much more to prayer. In our prayers, we should give our **worship** to God because He deserves our praise. Giving thanks is also an important part of prayer. And we can't forget to confess our sins and ask for His **forgiveness** as we pray.

. . . .

LEARN MORE: Philippians 4:6

IDEAS

RePeNTaNce

"I even preached to the people who are not Jews that they should be sorry for their sins and turn from them to God. I told them they should do things to show they are sorry for their sins."
ACTS 26:20

The apostle Paul wrote that repentance is the first part of salvation. Repentance includes telling God you have sinned and that you're sorry for it. You ask God to forgive you, and choose not to do that sin anymore.

King David repented when he prayed to the Lord, "Wash me inside and out from my wrong-doing and make me clean from my sin" (Psalm 51:2).

In the New Testament, John the Baptist preached that people needed to repent and turn to the Lord (Matthew 3:2). Jesus told the people, "Be sorry for your sins, turn from them, and believe the Good News" (Mark 1:15).

Being sorry for sins is not just something to do when you begin to follow Jesus. Throughout your Christian life, when you sin, tell God you're sorry, ask His forgiveness, and decide not to do that sin again.

LeARN MORe: Luke 15:7

168

RESURRECTION

If the dead are not raised, then Christ was not raised from the dead. If Christ was not raised from the dead, then what we preach to you is worth nothing. Your faith in Christ is worth nothing.
1 CORINTHIANS 15:13–14

. . . .

The apostle Paul wrote about how important Jesus' resurrection was. His victory over death means that those who believe in Him will be given new life after they die.

One time, when Jesus talked with Martha, He said that He was "the resurrection and the life." That was a way of saying Jesus is the Master over life and death. Then He brought Martha's brother Lazarus back from death.

After He rose from the dead Himself, Jesus spent 40 days with His followers before He went back to heaven. During that time, they could see for themselves that He was alive. Then they told others what they knew to be true.

God the Father has blessed all Christian believers with hope "because Jesus was raised from the dead" (1 Peter 1:3).

IDEAS

. . . .

LEARN MORE: John 11:25

SALVATION

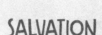

"There is no way to be saved from the punishment of sin through anyone else. For there is no other name under heaven given to men by which we can be saved."
ACTS 4:12

The apostle **Peter** spoke the words of Acts 4:12 to the Jewish religious leaders in **Jerusalem**. They questioned him and **John** the apostle about healing a man who was not able to walk. Peter explained to them that he could only do the **miracle** because of **Jesus**, who had risen from the dead.

Faith in Jesus is the only way to be free from **sin**. Salvation is knowing and believing that you are a sinner and that Jesus died to bring you new life. This new life is one that makes a relationship with a perfect **God** possible.

Jesus came to earth to bring salvation to a world of people who were lost and had no hope. This salvation is offered to all people. Jesus' death on the cross can cover all sin. But a person must choose to believe in Jesus and follow Him to receive the gift of salvation.

LEARN MORE: 1 Peter 1:8–9

SCRIPTURE

These Jews were more willing to understand than those in the city of Thessalonica. They were very glad to hear the Word of God, and they looked into the Holy Writings to see if those things were true.

ACTS 17:11

The people of Berea read through the Old Testament scriptures, wanting to make sure that what Paul said about Jesus being the Messiah was true. They wanted to learn more about God's written word.

"All the Holy Writings," Paul once said, "are God-given and are made alive by Him" (2 Timothy 3:16). Because the Bible is from God, it tells us how to live the way He wants us to.

The scriptures are full of wisdom to help us make good choices. They can help us feel better in sad times. They give us the knowledge we need to do what is right. And they show us how to want the praise of God more than the praise of people in everything we do.

LEARN MORE: Romans 15:4

IDEAS

SIN

If we live in the light as He is in the light, we share what we have in God with each other. And the blood of Jesus Christ, His Son, makes our lives clean from all sin.
1 JOHN 1:7

• •

Sin came into the world when Adam and Eve disobeyed God in the garden of Eden—and sin has been a part of the human race ever since. King David declared, "There is no one who does good" (Psalm 14:1).

When we disobey God and sin, we can't have everything God wants for our lives. But sin is not only doing what is wrong. We also sin when we don't do what we know is right. Jesus died for any sin we could ever do, but that doesn't ever make it okay to sin.

The punishment of sin is death. But God's generous gift is forgiveness for all of our sins and eternal life because Jesus died for us (Romans 6:23).

• •

LEARN MORE: James 4:17

SPIRITUAL FRUIT

But the fruit that comes from having the Holy Spirit in our lives is: love, joy, peace, not giving up, being kind, being good, having faith, being gentle, and being the boss over our own desires. The Law is not against these things.
GALATIANS 5:22–23

. . . .

In Galatians, there are nine words that describe the life of a person who follows Jesus. They show that Christians allow their lives to be controlled by the Holy Spirit. These nine qualities are known as the "fruit of the Spirit." Jesus said that other people will be able to see the power of God because of this "fruit" (Matthew 7:19–20).

The list begins with love, an attitude of unselfishness that puts others' needs before their own. Joy and peace in the Lord give believers strength in the good times and the bad times. Patience is the ability to keep being faithful to God. Kindness, gentleness, goodness, and self-control help us to show Jesus to all the people around us.

IDEAS

. . . .

LEARN MORE: James 3:17

SPIRITUAL GIFTS

But from your heart you should want the best gifts.
Now I will show you even a better way.
1 CORINTHIANS 12:31

Spiritual gifts are talents and abilities the Holy Spirit gives to people who love **Jesus.** They will make believers grow stronger in their **faith** and help other believers too.

The apostle **Paul** wrote about spiritual gifts in a letter to the Christians at Corinth. In the church, people were arguing about some gifts being better or more important than others. But Paul reminded them that all gifts are important. They should all be shared, no matter how small they may seem.

The gifts listed in the letter include teaching, faith, healing, doing miracles, prophecy, discernment, speaking in tongues, and interpreting tongues. They should all be used to help other Christians and show those who don't know Jesus how important it is to follow Him.

LEARN MORE: 1 Corinthians 12:1–31

IDEAS

TITHING

"Honor and thanks be to God Most High, Who has given into your hand those who fought against you." Then Abram gave Melchizedek a tenth of all he had taken.
GENESIS 14:20

Abraham gave a priest named Melchizedek ten percent (a "tithe") of what he had earned in battle. Abraham knew Melchizedek was also a worshipper of the one true God.

From then on, the Israelites, God's chosen people, would give a tithe to God. The law given to Moses said that they were to give ten percent of their crops and livestock as a special offering to God.

The New Testament does not say that a certain amount of giving is required. But those who love Jesus should be generous in sharing their money and possessions for God's work. Giving should be cheerful, from a heart of love for Jesus. He was the perfect example of generosity and sacrifice.

LEARN MORE: Luke 11:42

IDEAS

WORSHIP

*Come, let us bow down in worship. Let us get
down on our knees before the Lord Who made us.*
PSALM 95:6

The word *worship* comes from an old English word *worth-ship*. Worship is love and attention given to a person or thing. But only the God of the universe is truly worthy of worship.

Real worship has several parts to it. The first is adoration, or praise. We should come to God with joyful praise because He is so good and shows us mercy.

Another part of worship is thanksgiving. When we thank God for His goodness, we are saying that we know we need Him.

We also should think about God's holiness. We sin, but He never has. We have hurt Him when we've sinned against Him, but He forgives us when we ask Him to and loves us with His perfect love. He deserves all of our worship!

LEARN MORE: Psalm 99:5

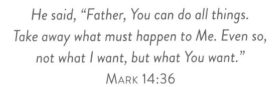

ABBA, FATHER

*He said, "Father, You can do all things.
Take away what must happen to Me. Even so,
not what I want, but what You want."*
MARK 14:36

. . . .

Abba is the name Jesus used for God the Father when He prayed in the garden of Gethsemane. It is an Aramaic word meaning "Father," similar to "Papa" in the English language.

The Jewish people usually would not have used this type of word for God. They thought of Him as someone who demanded more respect than that.

But it made sense for Jesus to call the Father *Abba*. As God's Son, He knew the Father more closely than anyone has ever known Him. Jesus Himself said, "I know My Father as My Father knows Me" (John 10:15). Through His death on the cross, Jesus made it possible for us to know God as a loving, forgiving Father too.

. . . .

LEARN MORE: John 10:37–38

NAMES OF GOD

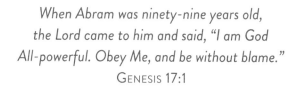

ALMIGHTY GOD

When Abram was ninety-nine years old,
the Lord came to him and said, "I am God
All-powerful. Obey Me, and be without blame."
GENESIS 17:1

. . . .

God had already promised Abram (later called Abraham) that He would make his descendants a great nation and give them a land of their own (Genesis 12:1–3; 13:15–17). But Abraham did not have any children, so he couldn't understand how that promise would happen.

By calling Himself "the All-powerful" in this verse, God was telling Abraham that He had the power to make miracles happen.

God can bless His people. And He has the power to make that blessing as big as He thinks best. The apostle Paul said, "God is able to do much more than we ask or think through His power working in us" (Ephesians 3:20).

. . . .

LEARN MORE: Revelation 15:3

ALPHA AND OMEGA

"I am the First and the Last.
I am the beginning and the end."
REVELATION 22:13

The name "Alpha and Omega" appears a few times in the Bible (see also Revelation 1:8, 11; 21:6). Alpha and omega were the first and last letters of the Greek alphabet—the language that most of the New Testament was written in. This name is a way of saying that Jesus is the beginning and the end of all things.

Jesus also said that He is the "First and the Last" (Revelation 1:17)—a name that means the same thing as Alpha and Omega. As the "First", He was with God the Father before the creation of the world (John 1:2). As the "last", He will be there when the earth has its end (Revelation 22:10–12).

LEARN MORE: Revelation 2:8

NAMES OF GOD

BELOVED SON

When Jesus came up out of the water, the heavens
opened. He saw the Spirit of God coming down and
resting on Jesus like a dove. A voice was heard from
heaven. It said, "This is My much-loved Son.
I am very happy with Him."
MATTHEW 3:16–17

• •

These verses tell what happened when John the Baptist
baptized Jesus. The heavens opened. The Holy Spirit
(looking like a dove) came down on Jesus. And God the
Father spoke up to say His "beloved Son" brought Him
joy. Now Jesus was ready to begin the work He was sent
to the world to do.

Because Jesus is God's much-loved Son, people
who believe in Him are also loved by God (Romans 1:7).
He dearly loves His children, those who have chosen to
follow Jesus and are doing what God the Father wants
them to do.

• •

LEARN MORE: 2 Peter 1:17

NAMES OF GOD

BREAD

*Then Jesus said to the people, "For sure, I tell you,
it was not Moses who gave you bread from heaven.
My Father gives you the true Bread from heaven."*
JOHN 6:32

In John 6, Jesus uses four different names for Himself,
all using the word *bread*. He calls Himself "Bread from
heaven" (verse 32), "Bread of God" (verse 33), "Bread
of Life" (verse 35), and "Living Bread" (verse 51).

Bread was a big part of the history of Israel. The Lord
kept His people alive in the wilderness after they escaped
from Egypt by sending a special bread called manna for
them to eat (Numbers 11:6–9).

Just as God sent food in the wilderness, He gives His
people what they need for life today. As the Living Bread
and the Bread of Life, Jesus gives the gift of eternal life
to everyone who takes Him into their life.

LEARN MORE: John 6:32–59

CHIEF CORNERSTONE

From now on you are not strangers and people who are not citizens. You are citizens together with those who belong to God. You belong in God's family. This family is built on the teachings of the missionaries and the early preachers. Jesus Christ Himself is the cornerstone, which is the most important part of the building.
EPHESIANS 2:19–20

A psalmist wrote, "The stone that was put aside by the workmen has become the most important stone in the building" Psalm (118:22). This was a prophecy about the coming Messiah, Jesus.

Jesus knew that many Jews would not believe that He was the Messiah. He told the disciples that His gift of salvation would be offered to the Gentiles, other people who would accept Him as Lord and Savior (Matthew 21:42–43).

In the stone buildings of Bible times, a cornerstone was used to hold stones together at the point where they came together in a corner. Jesus is the Chief Cornerstone, the firm base of our faith. Although some may choose to reject Him, He is the hope of the world and the only way to eternal life.

LEARN MORE: Isaiah 28:16

CHRIST

Simon Peter said, "You are the Christ,
the Son of the living God."
MATTHEW 16:16

. . . .

The disciple Peter knew that Jesus was the "anointed One" who had been sent into the world by God Himself. Jesus was the Son of God, the Messiah, the One who would deliver the Jewish people.

Jesus praised Peter for knowing He was God's anointed. Jesus was really the Messiah—but the Jews were expecting a warrior, not a spiritual Savior. Even people who heard Him preach did not think He was the Messiah that Old Testament scripture had promised. But Jesus did not come to earth to be a political king. He came to teach about the kingdom of God, to heal the sick, and to save the people from their sin.

. . . .

LEARN MORE: Luke 9:20

CREATOR

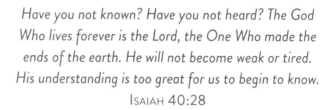

Have you not known? Have you not heard? The God Who lives forever is the Lord, the One Who made the ends of the earth. He will not become weak or tired. His understanding is too great for us to begin to know.
ISAIAH 40:28

. . . .

The prophet **Isaiah** could not believe that the people of **Judah** were turning away from the one true **God**. And they were worshipping false gods instead! The Creator God had made the universe by the power of His word. The idols had no power at all.

From the first chapter of the Bible, we learn important truths about God's **creation**. (1) He created our world from nothing. (2) He placed order and design into the universe. (3) Humans are the highest part of God's creation. (4) the Lord has given us the responsibility to take care of His world.

As Isaiah reminded the people of his nation, only our Creator God is worthy of our **worship**.

. . . .

LEARN MORE: Genesis 1:1–31

DOOR

"I am the Door. Anyone who goes in through Me will be saved from the punishment of sin."
JOHN 10:9

. . . .

A door is an opening or entryway into a place. By saying that He was the Door, Jesus meant He was the only way to salvation and eternal life.

In His Sermon on the Mount, Jesus talked about two doors (Matthew 7:13–14). The wide door, meaning the way of the world, was easy to walk through. It stands for doing whatever you want to do in life. But the narrow door, which means following Jesus and His teachings, is tougher to enter. It takes sacrifice to follow Jesus.

But don't forget that He said, "I am the Way and the Truth and the Life. No one can go to the Father except by Me" (John 14:6).

. . . .

LEARN MORE: John 10:7–10

EVERLASTING FATHER

For to us a Child will be born. To us a Son will be given.
And the rule of the nations will be on His shoulders.
His name will be called Wonderful, Teacher, Powerful
God, Father Who Lives Forever, Prince of Peace.
ISAIAH 9:6

. . . .

We usually talk about God as the Father and Jesus as the Son. But in this passage, Isaiah calls Jesus the "Father Who Lives Forever."

Jesus is one Person of the Trinity—God who is three Persons in One. This is very hard to understand, but we believe it by faith. Faith is believing in something we cannot completely know by ourselves. Because Jesus is God just as the Father is God, we know that Jesus was there before the beginning of the world. And He will not have any end. He lives forever, and He will love us forever!

. . . .

LEARN MORE: Isaiah 40:28

GOD

Thomas said to Him, "My Lord and my God!"
JOHN 20:28

. . . .

When "Doubting Thomas" finally saw Jesus after He rose from the dead, it was proof that everything he had heard was true. He also understood that Jesus was the Son of God. The verse above is one of the clearest statements that Jesus *is* God. Thomas, like all the other disciples, had lived and worked with Jesus for three years. They had seen His miracles and heard His teachings. They knew that Jesus had power. But it took them longer to understand that Jesus was actually God in a human body.

Being God and man at the same time, Jesus is both all-powerful and able to understand the struggles that we as people face.

. . . .

LEARN MORE: 1 Timothy 3:16

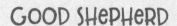
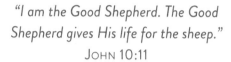

GOOD SHEPHERD

*"I am the Good Shepherd. The Good
Shepherd gives His life for the sheep."*
JOHN 10:11

Sheep are helpless animals that can't defend themselves against other animals that could harm them, like wolves and lions. Jesus calls His followers sheep and Himself the Shepherd who leads His flock (John 10:1–16).

The shepherd needs to constantly watch the sheep. If he doesn't, the sheep could wander away and get hurt. They need to be led from one place to another to find food and water. They need a good leader, one who will protect them and provide for them.

Jesus is our good shepherd. He loves us (His sheep) and is the best leader we could ever have. He will always protect us and provide for us.

LEARN MORE: Hebrews 13:20

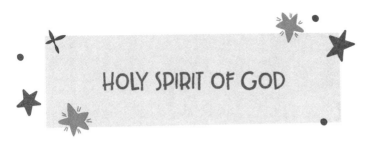

HOLY SPIRIT OF GOD

*Watch your talk! No bad words should be coming
from your mouth. Say what is good. Your words should
help others grow as Christians. Do not make God's Holy
Spirit have sorrow for the way you live. The Holy Spirit
has put a mark on you for the day you will be set free.*
EPHESIANS 4:29–30

. . . .

God's Holy Spirit can be made sad by the sinful actions
of Christians. This shows that the Holy Spirit is a person,
not just some kind of invisible force. Only a person can
experience emotions like sorrow, so the Spirit is a "He"
not an "it." He is as much a person as God the Father
and Jesus the Son.

If some actions by Christians make the Holy Spirit
sad, it's also true that certain attitudes and behaviors
bring Him pleasure. These include the fruits of the Spirit
in the apostle Paul's famous list in Galatians 5:22–23.

. . . .

LEARN MORE: John 14:26

NAMES OF GOD

I AM

Jesus said to them, "For sure, I tell you,
before Abraham was born, I was
and am and always will be!"
JOHN 8:58

. . . .

This name that Jesus called Himself, "I Am," is the same one God used for Himself when He spoke to Moses from the burning bush. Jesus was saying that He never had a beginning, and He will never have an end—He had always been and He would always be.

This statement made the Jewish religious leaders angry, so they picked up stones to throw at Jesus. That was the penalty for anyone who said they were equal with God (Leviticus 24:16). But Jesus was able to get away from them before they hurt Him. He would not be arrested and crucified until it was the right moment in God's plan.

. . . .

LEARN MORE: Exodus 3:14

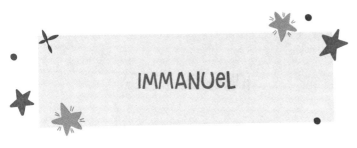

IMMANUEL

A young woman, who has never had a man, will give birth to a son. She will give Him the name Immanuel.
ISAIAH 7:14

This prophecy from Isaiah was fulfilled with the birth of Jesus (Matthew 1:22–23). The name Immanuel, meaning "God with us," was given to Jesus even before He was born by an angel who appeared to Joseph. He had promised to marry Mary but was concerned when he learned she was expecting a baby.

From the earliest pages of the Old Testament, God had promised to be with His people. These promises reached their peak in God's Son, Jesus Christ. He came to earth in the form of a man to show that God is for us in our sinful and helpless condition. As man, He understands our temptations and failures. As God, He can meet all these needs through His love and grace.

LEARN MORE: Hebrews 13:5

NAMES OF GOD

KING OF KINGS

"These kings will fight and make war with the Lamb. But the Lamb will win the war because He is Lord of lords and King of kings. His people are the called and chosen and faithful ones."
REVELATION 17:14

When **Jesus** comes back to earth, He will be wearing a banner with the phrase "King of Kings" on it. This name, telling of His power to rule over the whole earth, will be visible for everyone to see.

In Old Testament times, the title "king of kings" was given to a ruler with an area that covered a large territory. When Jesus returns, He will come as the ruler of the whole universe. If we have asked Him to be our Lord, we are subjects in His kingdom. He is King over our lives and King over the **church**.

LEARN MORE: Revelation 19:16

LAMB OF GOD

The next day John the Baptist saw Jesus coming to him. He said, "See! The Lamb of God Who takes away the sin of the world!"
JOHN 1:29

John the Baptist could have used any name for Jesus, but he chose "Lamb of God." Lambs were young sheep used as sacrificial animals in Jewish worship (Leviticus 14:11–13). At the very beginning of Jesus' ministry, John understood why Jesus came to earth and that He would be the sacrifice for all people.

On the night before He was crucified, Jesus and His disciples gathered to celebrate the meal together. It was a part of the Jewish festival of Passover. As Jesus passed the cup to the disciples, He said, "This is My blood of the New Way of Worship which is given for many. It is given so the sins of many can be forgiven" (Matthew 26:28).

LEARN MORE: Hebrews 9:12

LIGHT OF THE WORLD

Jesus spoke to all the people, saying, "I am the Light of the world. Anyone who follows Me will not walk in darkness. He will have the Light of Life."
JOHN 8:12

Jesus was sent by God the Father as a Savior for all people. This is one reason the religious leaders of that time didn't like Him. They didn't think it would be right for God to love the people of the world as much as He would love the Jewish leaders. They thought they knew all about how the Messiah would treat them when He came.

This problem is still here today. Some people think that Jesus would do certain things and wouldn't do other things. They believe they know exactly how He would act. But Jesus came for everyone—poor people, people with problems, and people who haven't heard of Him yet. He has come to be a Light for all, and His light will never get dim or go out.

LEARN MORE: John 9:5

MESSIAH

*The woman said to Him, "I know the Jews
are looking for One Who is coming. . . . When
He comes, He will tell us everything."*
JOHN 4:25

. . . .

Jesus let the Samaritan woman at the well in on a
secret—that He was the Messiah, the deliverer God had
promised to send to His people for hundreds of years.
She knew the "One Who is coming" would be able to
explain what she couldn't understand. But He told her
that He was the One she was waiting for.

The Jewish people expected their messiah to be a
political and military deliverer who would conquer Rome
and restore Israel. Jesus had come into the world as the
spiritual Messiah. They knew to expect His arrival; they
just didn't understand what His purpose would be.

. . . .

LEARN MORE: Daniel 9:25–26

NAMES OF GOD

POTTER

But now, O Lord, You are our Father.
We are the clay, and You are our pot maker.
All of us are the work of Your hand.
ISAIAH 64:8

. . . .

Throughout the Bible, God is pictured as a Master Potter ("Pot Maker" in the New Life Version). One time, the prophet Jeremiah watched a potter ruin a vase he was working on and decided to start over with the same lump of clay. Jeremiah compared the nation of Judah to this pottery reshaping process. Shape up, he told the people, or you will be reshaped by God's discipline.

Our human bodies are made of "the dust of the ground" (Genesis 2:7). But the apostle Paul said our "dirty" bodies still shine out the light of God (2 Corinthians 4:7). We should serve as witnesses of God's love to others.

. . . .

LEARN MORE: Jeremiah 18:2–6

REDEEMER

"But as for me, I know that the One Who bought me and made me free from sin lives, and that He will stand upon the earth in the end."
JOB 19:25

. . . .

The name *Redeemer* ("the One Who bought me") in Bible times described the nearest relative who would rescue a family member who was in trouble. So, if a person lost his property because of a debt, his *kinsman-redeemer* would buy it and give it back to the relative.

The prophet Isaiah wrote that God is the Redeemer who will come to the rescue of His people. What Isaiah and Job only hoped for has now happened. Any trouble we face will be taken care of by our Redeemer, the One who will rescue us. We can trust that Jesus will take care of us.

. . . .

LEARN MORE: Isaiah 59:20

ROCK

"There is no one holy like the Lord. For sure, there is no one other than You. There is no rock like our God."
1 SAMUEL 2:2

Hannah prayed this prayer when she brought her son Samuel to Eli the priest. God had answered her prayer and gave her a son, and she kept her promise to give him back to the Lord. She knew that God would always keep His promises.

The word *rock* describing God appears often in the book of Psalms. King David praised God for being his Rock of defense against King Saul.

"Rock," when used of God, doesn't mean a small stone, but a mountainside. There are large rock formations that can be seen throughout the land of Israel. Mountains of solid rock can protect from natural dangers and enemies, just as God the Father protects us and keeps us safe.

LEARN MORE: Psalm 94:22

SAVIOR

"There is no other God besides Me, a God Who is right and good, a God Who saves. There is none except Me."
ISAIAH 45:21

. . . .

A *savior* is a person who rescues someone from danger. This name is used for God in the Old Testament, and it often tells about God rescuing people from a bad situation. God sent plagues against the Egyptians when Pharaoh didn't allow the Israelites to leave his country. The plagues were God's way of saving His own people from slavery.

The New Testament talks less of people being saved from hard times and more of people being saved from their sins. Jesus came as Savior of the world. When He took our sins on Himself, He made it so that we can have a relationship with God.

. . . .

LEARN MORE: 1 Timothy 4:10

SHEPHERD

The Lord is my Shepherd. I will have everything I need.
He lets me rest in fields of green grass. He leads me
beside the quiet waters. He makes me strong again.
He leads me in the way of living right with Himself
which brings honor to His name.
PSALM 23:1–3

. . . .

David wrote this psalm toward the end of his life. He was praising God for being his Guide who would never fail him. Just like a shepherd leads his sheep to green pastures and quiet streams for food and water, the Lord had given David everything he needed. From his younger days as a shepherd boy all the way to when he became the king of Israel, God blessed David. David knew that God would always provide for him.

Like David, all of us need the Shepherd, who will be our Guide through life.

. . . .

LEARN MORE: Psalm 100:3

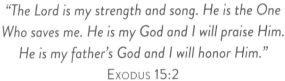

STRENGTH

"The Lord is my strength and song. He is the One Who saves me. He is my God and I will praise Him. He is my father's God and I will honor Him."
EXODUS 15:2

· ·

Moses and the Israelites sang Exodus 15:2 as a song of praise to the Lord. God had just saved them from the army of Egyptians who were chasing after them. The people had seen His power when He parted the waters of the Red Sea and allowed them all to walk safely through to the other side. It makes sense that Moses would call God his "strength."

Our God will always have enough strength to take care of His children anywhere, anytime. The prophet Isaiah said, "He gives strength to the weak. And He gives power to him who has little strength" (Isaiah 40:29).

· ·

LEARN MORE: Isaiah 40:28–31

NAMES OF GOD

STRONG TOWER

The name of the Lord is a strong tower. The man who does what is right runs into it and is safe.
PROVERBS 18:10

· ·

Towers were huge stone structures built above the walls of cities in Bible times. From the towers, the soldiers could protect the city, shooting arrows at the enemies on the other side of the wall.

The writer of Proverbs compares the Lord to one of these towers. His followers can find safety in Him, as He is the "strong tower." In a prayer of thanks, King David praised the Lord for serving as his "tower of salvation" against his enemies (2 Samuel 22:51). God used the idea of a tower to let the prophet Jeremiah know that He would strengthen him for the job of preaching His message to Judah (Jeremiah 1:18).

God will always be a "strong tower" for us, protecting us from any danger that could come our way.

· ·

LEARN MORE: Psalm 144:2

TRUTH

Jesus said, "I am the Way and the Truth and the Life. No one can go to the Father except by Me."
JOHN 14:6

Our world tells us that there are many different views of truth. Some people think they will find truth if they get a lot of money and possessions. Others think that getting knowledge leads to truth. Many people think that each person needs to find "their own truth," and that can be different for each one.

Jesus told Pilate that He had come into the world to "speak about the truth." But Pilate asked, "What is truth?" (John 18:37–38). The Truth—Jesus—was so close to Pilate that he could reach out and touch it, but he missed it because he didn't believe. As believers, we know the Truth. He will give us the help we need to learn what is right and what is wrong.

LEARN MORE: John 8:32

NAMES OF GOD

VINE

"I am the Vine and you are the branches. Get your life from Me. Then I will live in you and you will give much fruit. You can do nothing without Me."
JOHN 15:5

. . . .

The vine that Jesus was talking about was a grapevine. It had one main stem with several smaller stems going off in all directions. These smaller branches needed to depend completely on the main stem.

Jesus told His disciples that they should depend completely on Him as their Lord and Savior. He as "the Vine" would provide for them so they would grow "much fruit." And being a branch, or showing this spiritual fruit to those around them, could make others want to be followers of Christ too.

. . . .

LEARN MORE: Isaiah 5:1–2

NAMES OF GOD

WAY

Jesus said, "I am the Way and the Truth and the Life. No one can go to the Father except by Me."
JOHN 14:6

. . . .

The disciple Thomas was confused by Jesus' statement that He would leave soon after He rose from the dead (John 14:1–4). Thomas wanted to know how he and the other disciples could find Jesus after He left. Thomas was reminded that Jesus was the only "way" to heaven.

Sometimes thinking about heaven can make us forget about Jesus Himself. We wonder where heaven will be and what it will look like. We will never know the answers to these questions until we get there. But we do know the most important thing: Jesus is the only way to that wonderful place.

. . . .

LEARN MORE: John 14:1–7

WORD

The Word (Christ) was in the beginning.
The Word was with God. The Word was God.
JOHN 1:1

. . . .

The beginning of the Gospel of John teaches about Jesus as the eternal Son who was with God the Father before the world was created. Jesus was "in the beginning" (John 1:1) as the eternal Word and is the same God who was "in the beginning" (Genesis 1:1) creating the heavens and the earth.

Jesus is called "the Word" because He is where wisdom comes from, and He helps us to understand the Bible. Through His Word and His example from when He was on earth, we can learn about God and how we can live a life that honors Him.

. . . .

LEARN MORE: John 1:1–5

ANOTHER GREAT BOOK FOR BOYS!

God's Word makes boys brave. . .and you'll experience His unchanging truth firsthand in this daily devotional in the popular Brave Boys series. With each turn of the page, you'll see how God is working—every day—to grow you into the faithful, brave boy you were created to be.

Paperback / 978-1-64352-525-9 / $9.99